Also by Dan Hofstadter

T E M P E R A M E N T S

GOLDBERG'S
ANGEL

GOLDBERG'S ANGEL

An Adventure
in the Antiquities Trade

DAN HOFSTADTER

Farrar · Straus · Giroux
NEW YORK

FIRST EDITION, 1994

Library of Congress Cataloging-in-Publication Data
Hofstadter, Dan.
Goldberg's Angel: an adventure in the antiquities trade / Dan
Hofstadter.
p. cm.
1. Goldberg, Peg—Trials, litigation, etc. 2. Cyprus—Trials,
litigation, etc. 3. Antique dealers—Legal status, laws, etc.—
Indiana. 4. Cultural property, Protection of—Law and legislation—
Cyprus. 5. Icons, Greek—Indiana—Indianapolis. 6. Mosaics,
Greek—Indiana—Indianapolis. I. Title.
KF228.G47H64 1994 94-9801 CIP
364.1'62—dc20

To the Memory of
Presbytera Hariklia Frangos
1913–1993

Reverend Father Demetrios Frangos
1912–1994

Acknowledgments

My thanks for editorial help go to Robert Gottlieb, for publishing two sections of this story in *The New Yorker* and for making several sweeping and eminently useful suggestions; to Sara Lippincott, for her incisive early editing; to Liesl Schillinger, for her tireless research; to Elisabeth Sifton, for the insight and energy with which she has helped me to transform my tale into a book; and to Irene Skolnick, as always.

This text is so laden with proper names that I have refrained from mentioning in it all those fellow journalists who helped me behind the scenes. Chief among them is Mark Singer, who as a reporter for *The New Yorker* attended the *Cyprus v. Goldberg* trial in Indianapolis in late May and early June 1989, and who graciously allowed me to make use of his notes on that drama, which I myself missed. I wish, besides, to thank Özgen Acar, of *Cumhuriyet*, for sharing many observations with me; also Joe Gelarden and Steve Mannheimer of *The Indianapolis Star*; Geraldine

Norman of *The Independent*; Hasan Kahvecioğlu of *Ortam*; Makarios Drousiotis of *O Phileleftheros*; Chris Mitchell of Tartan TV, whose documentary film on the trial is mentioned toward the end of this book; and Karl E. Meyer of *The New York Times*, author of *The Plundered Past*. For information about the St. Louis auction scene I am indebted to the reporting of Tom Uhlenbrock of *The St. Louis Post-Dispatch*. The suggestions of Constance Lowenthal, of the International Foundation for Art Research, have been greatly appreciated.

For help with legal questions I thank Joe C. Emerson, Joseph H. Yeager, Sally F. Zweig, John David Hoover, Thomas C. Starns, Lawrence Kaye, Joe Cooper, Sarah Birn, and, above all, Thomas R. Kline of the Washington office of Andrews & Kurth.

For their invaluable translations I wish to thank Nurgün Güney, Andonis Mikrakis, and my friend Dr. George D. Frangos. It should be understood that since I speak neither Greek nor Turkish and do not engage in political reporting I have remained strictly neutral with regard to the Cyprus question. I have, however, received considerable help from both Turkish and Greek Cypriots alarmed by the wholesale looting of the northern part of the island. Many of my sources have wished to remain unnamed; to them I offer my mute but heartfelt gratitude. I also wish to thank Elias Eliades, Ambassador Petros Michaelides, Nicholas Kounoupias, Michael Kyprianou, Ergün Olgun, Osman Ertuğ, Ali Kanli, Hüsnü Feridun, Bora Atun, Osman Örek, Ahmet Erdengiz, Mustafa Akinci, and, most of all, the charming and ever hospitable Aytuğ Plümer.

I greatly appreciate the letter of introduction written for me by His Eminence Archbishop Iakovos, of the Greek Orthodox Archdiocese of North and South America; also the kind services of the late Reverend Father Demetrios Frangos.

I regret that words and names spelled with the dotless Turkish ı (as in *kadayıf* and Kanlı) have perforce been distorted by the requirements of American printing. I should also like to point out that the fictitious conversation found on pages 230–38 is based very largely on fact.

D.H.

GOLDBERG'S
ANGEL

Prologue

THE BAZAAR

Recently, while on a visit to Istanbul, I went—optimistically and, I suppose, blindly—to conclude some unfinished business in the Grand Bazaar, and before I realized that all business in that vast labyrinth is inherently unfinished, that I couldn't pull a switch there I'd know how to turn off, I got interested in the story of the place. I decided to play a little scholarly hooky in the Istanbul Library, on nearby Soğukçeşme Street, and as the rain beat upon its tall windows I discovered what I might have suspected: that the story of the bazaar, like the bazaar itself, is all fiction and fantasy and dream. For writers who have tried to chart its ways, for the Turk Çelik Gülersoy as for the Frenchman Théophile Gautier, it teems not so much with products or people as with possibilities. It leads you down conversational alleys, up flights of poetical stairs, and the reason is that it offers the ideal setting for something as old as commerce itself: the lyricism of the market, the ballyhoo of the stalls, the freedom to jabber at a daring remove from the hard world of fact outside. Of course, the bazaar is not what it once was—today it displays all the crudity of contemporary life—but I learned that its tolerance for inflated speech has for centuries been pretty much the same.

Of all the old traveler's reports, the one by Edmondo De Amicis pleased me the most. A master of the personal essay, De Amicis set down his observations in a book entitled *Constantinople*, which was published, in Italian, in 1877. He tells us that he approached the bazaar from the district of the Yeni Cami, or New Mosque, a short distance to the north. He passed first through the long tunnel-vault of the Egyptian Market, which specialized, as it still does, in condiments, peppers, pistachios, candied fruits, pickled plums, rose water, fenugreek, ewe's-milk cheese, loukoum, halvahs, apricot papers, and every variety of savory paste and powder. The material lent itself to his literary manner, which relied on an ample inventory of exoticisms. He was shown wares that went "to color the faces and figures of the odalisques, to perfume rooms and baths and breaths and beards and dishes, to reinvigorate exhausted pashas, to calm unhappy wives, to stupefy smokers, to spread dreams, intoxication, and forgetfulness over the interminable city." Forging on, he walked through a zone of coppersmiths' shops and foul-smelling taverns until he came to the Beyazit Gate of the bazaar itself, and it is here that his description exactly matches what one finds at the same spot today.

The bazaar proved to be not an ordinary covered market but an enormous medieval burg that was wholly devoted to trade; yet it allowed no echo of the hubbub within to escape its encircling wall. By the gate stood a motley crew of self-appointed "drago-men," or ropers, speaking many languages and won-derfully adept in the art of detecting a traveler's nationality; these leeches instantly clung to those vis-itors who seemed most likely to be parted from their money. Then, as now, you could not shake them off without making an embarrassing scene, and so you allowed yourself to be led through the bowels of the bazaar to some glittering shop, at whose doorway your guide would dissolve into the crowd.

The Grand Bazaar was a "real city," De Amicis noted, with its own squares, crossroads, mosques, and fountains. Wandering about inside it, he was amazed at how easily he lost track of time. In the market of arms and armor a man might haggle for three hours over the price of an engraved scimitar, then swear that only three minutes had passed; or he might feel that he had spent the better part of his life lingering over the swansdown and raveled silk of the slipper stalls. The perfumers' souk seemed infinite, kaleido-scopic, and De Amicis painted it in deep purple shades: "Here are found the famous seraglio pastilles for perfuming kisses, the capsules of odiferous gum which the robust girls of Chio make for the reinforce-ment of the mouths of the soft Turkish ladies . . ." In a quarter of textile and clothing booths, waylaid by mountains of Baghdad brocades and scarves "as light as sunset clouds," he remarked a vast selection of fabrics of every sort, and more sorts, too, than he had ever imagined could exist. He noted types and sub-types, categories within categories; he observed that the spinners of gold thread had a whole neighbor-hood to themselves. At this time, despite the recent dress reform of Sultan Mahmut, the costume of the

Ottoman woman was still a mysterious and intriguing affair for Europeans, and the Italian stood "in open-mouthed wonder" as he surveyed the cascades of intimate feminine garments. "Here may be found, one by one, each part of the Turkish lady's dress," he marveled, "from the mantle, green, orange, or purple, that covers the whole person, down to the silken chemise, the gold-embroidered kerchief, and the satin girdle on which no eye of man is permitted to fall, save that of the husband or eunuch." What De Amicis felt is what travelers have always felt in the toils of this vast emporium: that the endless segmentation of the retail assortment, the minute, almost museumlike classification of items for sale, plays havoc with your sense of the passage of time. Your memory is overcharged by the wilderness of goods, overstimulated by the splintering of the shopping circuit into a thousand highly colored moments, and amid so many cries and so many pleas, so many additions and subtractions and guarantees and explanations, your hold on reality imperceptibly weakens and you yield to the sensuality of delay.

And, well, why not? For the Grand Bazaar is perhaps the world's finest example of the architecture of delay, a veritable wild-goose chase in stone. More addictive than an opium den, more magnetic than a penny arcade, it seems designed to detain and inveigle the shopper, to entangle him in a tapestry of merchandise. If, gawking about this maze, you eventually notice certain recurrent features—maybe a coffeehouse, or a marble fountain, or a stairway climbing to a tiny mosque whose tall wooden pulpit rises like a monitory finger over the milling crowd—you cannot without days of concerted effort grasp how to make your way from landmark to landmark, since you are constantly subject to repetition without direction, pattern without orientation. Though the market has always been run by males, it feels to males a feminine space—unmappable, seductive, perilous.

Such a warren of alleyways, courtyards, cul-de-sacs, galleries, and catwalks necessarily eludes graphic description, yet it is not so inchoate as to frighten you off. Inside the actual covered bazaar—for the whole market district is only partially roofed—are two large *bedestens,* or fortified trading arcades, which during the Ottoman centuries housed strongrooms for the protection and display of gold and silver objects, valuable jewelry, expensive brocades, and gold thread. These bedestens form the recognizable core of the bazaar; around them, but still within the covered part of the market, are hundreds of shop-lined pedestrian "streets" whose names reflect their function in those bygone days when each business or craft occupied its own well-defined zone. There is a Spoon Dealers' Street, a Mirror Dealers' Street, a Gilders' Street, a Quilt Makers' Street, a Scissors Sellers' Street; but today, when so much of the market is given over to inferior dry goods and souvenirs, only the antique dealers and the dealers in precious metals (who are numerous and important) can be said to occupy separate quarters of their own.

Almost encircling the covered market is an area of ancient caravanseries, or khans, that serve as warehouses and workshops, and generally these khans maintain the Turkish custom of segregating the trades, so that even today you can easily distinguish a khan used as a silversmith's atelier from one used as a garment sweatshop or a depot for yard goods. Commonly hidden at the far end of sewerlike vaults, these quadrangular buildings enclose spacious courts graced with arcades, porticos, and curiously shaped windows; as your gaze travels higher, these features grow ever smaller, until you discover dwarfish loggias whose doors frame scenes like genre paintings of workmen making intricate molds or hunching over vessels of chased silver. The khans are like specimens behind glass of the old occupations: each one seems given over to some particular odor and visual mood, so that, for instance, in the Kalçi Khan you whiff the pungent stench of molten silver alloys, hear the din of tiny hammers, and notice that everything is coated with a monochrome of sepia soot, as if the whole court were changing into a vintage photograph before your eyes.

No matter how well you think you know the bazaar, your image of it crumples once you set foot inside it. Even those who work there grasp only what bears on their pocketbooks, and I've listened with amusement as merchants or shop clerks, acquaintances of mine, have refused even to enter certain dark passages or half-hidden courts, insisting that they would feel like trespassers if they took another step. Some isolated portions of the bazaar, which you may enter only by ducking under a low arch, force you to thread your way along narrow balconies or through corridors sunk below street level, and when at length you come out into the open, onto the broken tiles of some steeply slanting pavement or under the overhang of some disjointed balcony, you may well discover that you have ended up in a sealed-off court, or back at your point of departure in a dungeon-like alley where the flatbread seller and the cucumber man stare at you quizzically from behind their heaped-up barrows.

Finding your bearings would be easier if the bazaar folk were stationary, but they aren't, because the Turkish shopkeepers retain one curious vestige of their nomadic heritage and that is the habit of taking coffee or lunch or tea-with-sweets whenever they want and wherever they are, with the consequence that runners dangling overloaded trays dash at most hours through the crowded walkways, leaving off or picking up collections of little glasses and dishes, while migrating watersellers bob up and down, filling cups with flavored water from the ornate urns on their backs, and skullcapped vendors wheel vitrines of stewed figs and milk puddings and kadayifs and baklavas along endless rows of almost identical booths, until at day's end, in the glancing light, the doorways are littered with pudding plates and the merchants wash tea glasses in the marble fountains and a gnome-like man strapped to a huge wooden box tramps along singing the virtues of his beautiful and most useful paper napkins.

Perhaps it has taken you all day to realize why you are here, but the bazaar folk knew it from the start. Exhausted yet animated by a feverish curiosity, you fall into the hands of a particularly sympathetic and charming young roper, who, while telling you of his chief interest in life, which is to obtain a scholarship to study mechanical engineering at Brigham Young University, happens to lead you into a dark grotto lined with slanting columns, shimmering with arched and dentellated niches, and overgrown with the tendrils of innumerable creepers in nameless shades of indigo, aubergine, and celadon; through the whole scene dances in a hundred shapes and guises the figure of an angular lady with her hands on her hips. You are, of course, in a carpet shop, and these architectural designs and vegetal efflorescences belong to the mazy laps and overlaps of a hundred different rugs— the ubiquitous lady being none other than Elibelinde, the Anatolian goddess of fertility and favored motif of the Türkmen weavers. Your straying into this place with the eloquent young roper, and the subsequent spell of bargaining in an indeterminate stretch of dream-time, will one day occupy the center of your tale of the bazaar—it will be the speaking conch in your prayer rug of memory—and this the dealers already know, because a visit to a rug shop (or an antiquarian bookshop, or an icon shop, or an armor shop—the nature of the merchandise scarcely matters) has always formed the inmost kernel of every Westerner's account of a trip to the bazaar (including those of Théophile Gautier and Edmondo De Amicis).

This obligatory visit, which has all the compulsion of a nightmare, always starts with your "not intending to buy," as you frankly explain to the five amiable merchants who are just now rising to greet you; they reply (in whatever language you happen to speak, for they have been everywhere and studied everything and have subtle estimations of Harley Street surgeons and the string section of the Wiener Philharmoniker) that nobody who has darkened their threshold has ever wished to do anything but educate himself, yet every civilized land counts many contented customers from their shop. At once splendid rugs are unfurled, each telling through a salesman's mouth its half-truth; and the haggling process has begun. This process is too well known to warrant any but the briefest reiteration here: the arrival of coffee or apple tea, the flattering compliments and general softening-up patter, the parading of items that seem like near-relations to one another, the introduction of bewildering complications regarding the mode of payment, the lightning consultation of digital calculators, the inevitable interlude of despair, the palms-up gestures and wounded-animal looks, the final concessive removal of the superb piece in the back office, hanging over the proprietor's own desk, which was not really for sale but will be made available to a person of your evident distinction—these fixed phases in the ceremonial exchange have been recounted in countless traveler's tales.

Your one probable misapprehension is to think that this is a debate between you and the merchants, for it is not, since they know your arguments in advance; really, it is a debate within each party over how courteous or ruthless to be, a dialogue between politeness and predation. You must decently assent to the expertise of the dealer and the beauty of his wares; he must decently grant that you are not made of money and are capable of elementary astuteness; neither party can concede too much, however, or there will be no advantage, no sale. The tradition of pitiless bargaining is often thought to be native to Muslims, but according to students of such matters it is not. De Amicis speaks of the "silent Turk, seated cross-legged upon his carpet at the entrance to his shop," resigned to destiny; the loud voice, the peremptory gesture, the fawning entreaty—these were the property of non-Muslim merchants. Most adept of all hagglers were the "Levantines," who were not, in the jargon of

Istanbulites, persons of Eastern Mediterranean extraction but, rather, the descendants of Westerners, Frankish traders, and others, who had undergone orientalization. "To what people do these belong?" De Amicis wondered. "No one knows. By dint of talking in every language, they have lost their primitive accent; by dint of acting comedy all day long, they have changed the physiognomical features of their race; they are of any country they please for the moment . . ." The Levantines have all but vanished from the bazaar, but those who have supplanted them show the same characteristics. They are consummate performers, chameleons, vaudevillians, and view the exercise of their métier as a kind of theatrical performance demanding flowery speeches, stage whispers, confidential asides, a whole mumming vocabulary of gestures and winks.

And yet, and yet: is not the final handshake, that instant when goods and payment symbolically change hands, one of the blindest in the life of the soul—a moment of terrible taunting laughter in the dark? Especially with purchases involving large sums of money, who knows how much spiritual arm wrestling, how much seduction and abandonment and intimate humiliation, go into that meeting of skin with skin, which usually by its very nature signifies the defeat of one being and the triumph of another?

On my last visit to Istanbul, I spent five days searching vainly through the bazaar, and each day it grew clearer to me that the whole obsessive quest—the delays, detours, crossways, and forked alleys, the false recognitions, the mocking reappearance of faces and landmarks, and, finally, the inevitable moment of confessing that I was completely lost—was like a spatial analogue to the bargaining process. The topographical maze of alternative routes and dead ends parallels the situational maze of trying to strike a deal with someone who is infinitely cannier than you, someone who moves with keener instincts and superior foresight across a mental board game marked with innumerable arrows and subject to ever-shifting imponderables: rates of exchange, repair costs, "brother" or "cousin" discounts, proofs of authenticity or antiquity. What defeats your capacity to see your way forward is precisely what has been enchanting you all along, namely the siren song of the Oriental mode of display, the fabulously complex subdivision of commerce.

Look around you: that tea seller waiting in his glimmering tiled cell behind those rows of glasses in which tall spoons are standing—he dispenses nothing but tea. That saucer washer plying his trade in that stand the size of a telephone booth—he washes nothing but saucers. The barber snipping and combing in that minuscule one-seat barbershop dresses only men's hair, and the vendor standing behind that tiny vitrine hawks only meat pastries, and never more than twenty at a time. That man with the hammer sells only hand-sawn plywood shoe heels (he will gladly nail on a pair for you) and that other man with the small box hanging from his neck sells only leatherette watchbands. Amid the slanting sunbeams and dancing motes of the Stamboul Yenni Tcharchi, a market-within-a-market that is glassed in like a hothouse and traversed by an indoor bridge of filigree ironwork, bent silhouettes come and go, bearing cartons of defective cellular phones, loose sunglass lenses, acrylic brooches, mismatched pajama buttons, all the flotsam of industrial civilization, while somewhere else, a few alleys distant (I was taken to him once but will never find him again), a little old man collects and refurbishes all the bazaar's broken-down weighing equipment—scales, pans, hooks, weights, and chains—which he stores in a windowless, airless room. For me that tangle of brassware, intricate, hypnotic, Medusa-like, with its streaks of serpentine sheen and innumerable dull staring highlights, will always serve as the most memorable image and summation of the Grand Bazaar, a place in which time is infinitely elastic and anything is convertible into anything else.

1

It embarrasses me to admit that there was a time, not long ago, when I depended for most of my information on a single person. It embarrasses me as a reporter and as a man. That all my evolving sense of the business world, of the way things happen and the way they don't, of what you can and cannot expect to get away with, should be determined by one woman, even a woman so far out of the ordinary—it now seems a little incredible. And yet, I confess, that's how it was.

Knowing nothing, craving to know everything, I wanted to lay bare the mechanism of a fantastically complicated affair, to grasp its perverse intricacy, to feel the magic of handshakes and the radiance of talismans, to know which idols to beseech and which to flout. I also wanted to understand why the evil eye, which I'd always thought of as a silly superstition or maybe a name for other people's bad luck, seemed to be peering slowly around in my direction. All these things I wanted; and that is why, for a while, I relied on the extraordinary woman.

Her name is Peg—Peg Goldberg. Sometime after she got involved in this affair, she started referring to herself as "little Peg," though that's not necessarily how anyone else would think of her. "Consider it this way," she would say to me every once in a while. "Here's me, little Peg, taking on all those men in black collars." Which was true—I couldn't deny it—but *little* Peg? When she laughs, I mean really laughs, you fear for the windows in their sashes. Peg is a big woman, with a big woman's need not to be humbled, and for a long time she devoted all her energy to getting out of the plight she was in. About six years ago, some picturesque characters dragged her into it. "Lovely people, huh?" she used to exclaim to me. "Charming people!"

Well, some of them *are* charming, which is part of the problem. If they weren't so charming, so magnetic, a lot of bad things might not have happened to her. They belong to the worldwide network of antiquities dealers, whose calling it is to buy very old things and to sell them to (on the whole) very new people—the newly rich, or buyers from new and rich institutions. They hawk sarcophagus fragments and cinerary urns, kneeling Niobids and canopic jars, and for some reason—perhaps because of all that Peg has told me—I picture them rummaging in vaults and sepulchral chambers, like antiquities traders in pulp novelettes. Beckoning, cajoling, caressing their treasures, they have some of the dustiness and some of the glamour of those bygone fictional people.

What Peg now knows—what all canny buyers in the international antiquities bazaar know—is that every one of those cracked or corroded treasures, every one of those porphyry reliefs and embalmed heads of saints, has its own voice, its own tale to tell. You or I may not be able to hear it, but somewhere there is someone who can. The strange and sinister thing is that many of these tales are untruths, for certain objects can lie. They can lie about what they are or who owns them or where they came from, which is only to say that their sellers have tagged them with a false identity or false provenance. Like everything that is beautiful in this world, the noblest of these objects move toward the light, away from the crypt and the worm, yet many of their purveyors have it as a cardinal rule to operate solely in darkness. Secrecy is their watchword and, so they feel, their incontestable right. Their sources and accounts are shrouded in gloom, and if anyone should ask them the true origin of something, they will turn away with an inscrutable look, a strict closure of the heart, like a person slamming a door. Often, it seems, they do not wish to have faces at all.

Peg is a woman betrayed by a secret—or at least that's how she sees it. Six years ago, as a fledgling art dealer knowing next to nothing of the antiquities trade, she went to Europe and rather too swiftly bought four Early Christian devotional mosaics, each about two feet square. She paid a little more than a million dollars for them, in cold cash—money she had borrowed from an Indiana bank. She believed that she had obtained good title to the mosaics, but in less than a year the men in black collars appeared and claimed that the holy icons were theirs and had been so for more than a thousand years. They were prelates of the Autocephalous Greek Orthodox Church of Cyprus, and through the agency of the Republic of Cyprus and that country's American lawyers they demanded that the pieces be surrendered into their custody. They said that the mosaics were actually war booty, illegally torn, along with several companion pieces, from the little church of Panagía Kanakariá, in the village of Lythrankomí, some time after the Turkish seizure of northern Cyprus, in 1974. This was the secret Peg had not known. But she did not give them the mosaics, and so they sued her in Indianapolis, her hometown.

The trial took place late in the spring of 1989. It was held in the porticoed federal courthouse on Ohio Street, downtown, which has its own mosaics, dating from the turn of the century, over the grand stairways inside. The courtroom was packed, the international press was in attendance, and a parade of exotic witnesses enlivened the six days of proceedings. The most impressive of these was Father Pavlos Maheriotis, an abbot representing the Church of Cyprus, who, after testifying that the Church owned the Kanakariá mosaics and had never authorized anyone to remove them, listened impassively to the other witnesses with his hands cupped on his gold-crested pastoral staff and his white-streaked black beard flowing down over his black habiliments. The legal issues were complex, and the spectators heard impassioned discourse by able lawyers and erudite experts. Peg herself was heroic in scale—it was as if one of the statues outside had deigned to step off its pedestal and join the gathering. *Cyprus v. Goldberg* promised to be a historic event—the most important postwar litigation between a people trying to recover a fragment of their patrimony and an individual of good repute who had paid coin of the realm for the same fragment.

Peg Goldberg was then living where she still lives,

on the northern outskirts of Indianapolis, and so was her former friend Bob Fitzgerald. Bob was also involved in the mosaics affair, and the mere fact that the two of them should have left their Midwestern suburban houses and journeyed to Europe and returned home with a considerable part of the apse of a Byzantine church says something about Indianapolis itself. If you drive out to Peg's by way of Eighty-sixth Street, the roadside strip looks like any other in America, all rectangles and big, bright letters, and you could probably spray-paint a copy along some highway in Tennessee or Arizona that would fit right in with its new surroundings. The northern suburbs are flung out over the gentle Indiana farmland. The houses look nondescript until you reach the remoter towns, like the one where Peg lives, but there, in the Georgian ranch houses and shingle-style Norman châteaus springing up in the midst of tilled fields, you sense a hankering for the historical. Gradually you realize that the main drags impose a commercial conformity that doesn't necessarily seep back into the big chunks of real estate lying hidden from the driver's eye.

Peg, who is in her middle fifties, stands well over six feet tall and has close-cut light-blond hair. She wears rugby shirts and jeans and sensible shoes, and she lives in a huge white house with vast interior spaces, like a big city loft washed up on a cornfield. Her voice is a limber mezzo, fit for song or stage; she also has an entertainer's ear for common speech, so that if she has to run an important errand it is "tattooed on her forehead," and if she favors a local restaurant it "serves the best bread in captivity." Her features are regular, her eyes smallish and high-set, and her expressions shift rapidly and sometimes overlap, a pucker of doubt claiming one half of the face while a smile fades from the other. She dresses in bold colors and likes bright-colored art; there's a kind of integrity to the unrelenting forwardness of the pictures hanging in her house. Peg lives with six cats and four dogs—she calls them "my wuffs and meows"—which she rescued from vagrancy, and her individuality concentrates itself in an affection for all creatures stray, derelict, maimed, or in revolt. Readily trotting out dismissive witticisms for every established profession—for physicians, lawyers, clerics, administrators, and any other group you might name—she is an American original, a deep-dyed Midwestern nonconformist. From the moment you meet her, you feel that like all nonconformists she possesses an instinctive attitude of sometimes mute, sometimes unwitting protest against the order of the world. To her friends' amusement and her critics' irritation, she wears an air of absolute, never-failing competence, as if to say that here, in case you need one, is a Swiss army knife of a gal.

Peg's father was Jewish—a plant manager—but she was brought up in her mother's Protestant faith. Her maternal grandmother was very devout, and her great-great-grandfather had been a circuit rider who brought the Good News to the back roads of Indiana. Their denomination was the Disciples of Christ, which in the early nineteenth century broke away from the Presbyterian Church and later won a strong following in the Bible Belt. The founding ministers of the Disciples of Christ objected to all hierarchies and dogmas that stood between man and his Maker; they advocated a return to the pure Christianity of Jesus' own lifetime and stressed the believer's ability to re-create the nearness to God that the apostles had experienced. These were among the teachings that Peg absorbed at Sunday school in the 1940s; she also took music lessons, and by the age of fifteen she was playing the organ for her church and for the Sunday services at a state park in the rolling hills of Owen County, in southern Indiana, where she grew up. In grade after grade, she was the brightest and the tallest. She tried in her early teens to pass unnoticed, keeping her mouth shut and standing behind other children, but these dodges didn't work very well, and she gave them up one day when her best friend sat her down and advised her to be who she was. "I could try to be all sorts of things," Peg told me. "But unobtrusive? Unh-unh."

Peg breezed through Indiana University on an academic scholarship; she was elected to Phi Beta Kappa and received a B.A. *cum laude* in sociology and psychology. Fairly certain that she wanted to enter the field of mental-health care, she enrolled in 1961 in the M.A. program at Christian Theological Seminary, a highly rated Indiana graduate school affiliated with the Disciples of Christ, where she studied psychological counseling, with a minor in ethics. As a child, Peg had been taught that religion has a lot to do with looking out for your fellow man, and by now she had become conscious of how much poverty and social distress there was in Indianapolis. The civil-rights movement had begun, and many of the teachers and students at C.T.S. were speaking out in defense of progressive causes. Though by this time Peg's Christian faith had given way, her moral sense was strengthened by the atmosphere around her and by the wave of reformism sweeping the country.

Sometime after receiving her M.A., she became a caseworker for the Marion County welfare department and began to specialize in helping battered or sexually abused children. She often found herself in court, called to give testimony about mistreated youngsters; there she discovered that judges and functionaries were seldom interested in what she had to say, and after a while she began to suspect that they were not sympathetic to poor people at all. It was the beginning of a period of abrasion between Peg and the bureaucracy. In 1970, she became the director of special services for the county's retarded citizens, a job she retained for eight years; in the words of one of her old progressive friends, she was "a worker in the vineyard," a thorn in the side of those who did not share her ardent desire to redesign the world. She once admitted to me, as we were tooling around northside in her Plymouth Voyager, that she had often felt misunderstood by her co-workers. They were surprised that she was so unsentimental about her charges, that there was never a catch in her throat. "They wanted to see tears," she told me, "but I didn't want to cry. I wanted to fight back, to get something done."

Then for two years Peg held the post of director of programs for a home for the retarded and the disabled. In 1980, however, she left, on account of a personal conflict, and could not get another job in her field. Her sense of her worth was deeply hurt, and she also admitted to herself that she felt too burned-out to go on trying to reform Indianapolis. She was a sixties person, and these were the 1980s.

Peg was now forty-one years old, and she had no money; she'd never been interested in money. For a while, she played the organ for the crowds at a shopping mall and did other odd jobs. Ever resourceful, however, she had begun to notice something hopeful about her life, like a bright promise concealed in the foreground. Though she couldn't draw or paint, Peg had long been interested in the visual arts and had assembled a small art collection, consisting mostly of prints and drawings. Sometimes she swapped or sold things, or informally represented friends of hers whose work she admired, and it occurred to her now that if she got an entry-level position at a local gallery she might soon acquire enough practical experience to open a gallery of her own. Within a short time, she found work in such a shop, selling posters and answering the phone, and all the while she observed how the business was run. She thought that as a gallery owner she could continue to help people—there were some talented artists around who sorely needed help—and at the same time have a go at making some serious money and deriving some pleasure from life, which, she now confessed to herself, she hadn't done for a long time. Soon she began to sell inexpensive works of art, dealing out of her house, and the venture went astonishingly well. In 1986, she expanded the house, turning much of it into exhibition space, and she also took on a partner, the former art instructor at the home for the retarded she had helped to run.

Peg became a familiar figure in her suburban neighborhood, and in the spring of 1986 she ran for the office of county commissioner. It was an unlikely campaign—here was this flamboyant art dealer named Goldberg who looked like Brünnhilde and had a bee in her bonnet about cronyism—but she won. In the process, she was aided by a neighbor, somewhat older than she was, named Otto N. Frenzel III (his friends called him Nick), who lived in a mansion over the hill. A scion of one of Indiana's richest banking families, he would one day enable her to borrow a million-odd dollars to purchase four Early Christian mosaics.

In 1981, while Peg was still working for the small poster-and-print business, a barrel-chested, silver-haired man named Bob Fitzgerald started coming into the shop now and then to have some framing done. He wore Levi's and moccasins and a shirt open at the neck, and he spoke with the deep, slightly reedy voice of an old-time country-and-Western singer. He said he was an art dealer who had spent his life searching for beautiful artifacts all over the world, especially in the jungles and highlands of Latin America, and that he had settled in Indianapolis on account of a few very rich clients. He invited her over to the condo he had recently bought, and when she dropped in on him one day she found rooms full of pre-Columbian, African, and Oceanic pieces—Nazca pottery and Senufo idols and masks from New Guinea and lots of gold objets d'art. Their well-traveled owner told her that he had left home very young to work as an animal dealer—he adored exotic animals—before becoming, as she understood it, a sort of background picker for some of the best antiquities and primitive-art galleries on both coasts. In sustained conversation he struck her as mercurial and high-strung—she later came to think of him as "an adult version of a hyperactive child"—yet also funny and teasing, and a spellbinding raconteur. She noticed, with some distaste, that he excelled at chatting up young girls.

There seemed to be a core of genuine feeling to Bob—he doted on his elderly, ailing mother and on his and other people's pets—but his education was discernibly faulty. After a year or so, Peg decided that Bob might be somewhat dyslexic; he was always saying things like "I can't seem to find my glasses—could you just read this to me?" and she never once saw him open a book. He had, all the same, a vast fund of knowledge, which came, invariably, in the form of inside dope: Bob in his condo was Bob on two phones at once, waiting for a third call to light up, his handsome, actorish head silhouetted against a giant television screen that flickered nonstop with Sandinistas and Republican fund-raisers and leveraged-buyout kings.

Some pretty important people turned up at the condo, and when, a year or so after Peg met him, Bob opened a fancy steakhouse in the neighborhood, the important people turned up there, too. They bought art from him for distinguished collections; they bought for well-known museums. Bob, who could be attentive and affectionate to his friends, might haggle for hours with ruthless obstinacy, and Peg remembers that she sometimes came away from those meetings of museum people and big out-of-town dealers with vituperative phrases ringing in her ears: *Don't you try to play games with me. Don't you try to jerk me around.* This bloody-minded business style put her off, but she was fascinated by the beautiful pieces and the high numbers, and she was glad to help Bob out now and then by gathering information or researching the provenance of some potential purchase. Bob had a taste for long shots, and sometimes Peg—he called her "good ol' Peg" on such occasions—would discover that the latest object of his desire had been skulking around the market for six or seven years with danger signs hanging all over it. Later, when Peg took up dealing, Bob told her that she had a lot of talent and should forget about the "low-end stuff" she was pushing and go for the big-time pieces. To be a dealer, he said, you had to take the sportsman's point of view, and if you couldn't steel yourself to play for high stakes, you'd probably never get anywhere. But Peg decided to ignore Bob's baiting—in part because she didn't care much for his end of the business, and in part because she was still feeling her way slowly forward. She was tickled, though, when he showed her how he could close his eyes and tell by merely touching or sniffing a piece—some Peruvian figurine, say—exactly what it was, and she knew in her bones that one day she would be able to do the same, though certainly not with the same line of merchandise.

Wherever you go in the Indianapolis suburbs you smell air freshener—it's in stores, malls, hotels, and cabs, and maybe even in flower beds—and though you might think this air-freshener atmosphere would drive out people like Peg and Bob, strangely enough it does not. Bob defeats air freshener, because he more or less chain-smokes, cradling a cigarette in his muscular hand most of the time, even when he's driving his gray Jaguar. Bob has wavy hair, which he wears swept back with gel, a few strands drooping over his tawny forehead. His eyes are large and brown, and his elegant bone structure is still visible under a mask of middle-aged suet. He's in his late fifties, with a laughing-cavalier smile that carries a long way. Once, when we were ripping up Eighty-sixth Street in the Jag, a car full of pretty young girls pulled alongside, all smiling and waving at Bob.

Bob talking is almost show biz, like a man doing an improv sketch of himself. I spent some time with him in Indianapolis a year or so after the trial, talking with him in his condo or in his car or at his favorite tavern. He leads with one shoulder as he regales you with traveler's tales, looks down over the shoulder with his coffee-colored eyes, sizes you up, gets a line on you faster than you can get a line on him. Every once in a while he halts in mid-sentence or throws you a question, peering into you with eyebrows raised, poised like the hands of a timpanist awaiting his entrance. "I'm a hustler," he says, to disarm you.

Bob told me one time that he was a Depression baby whose father had a drinking problem and split up with Bob's mother when Bob was a toddler. Bob's maternal grandparents brought him and his mother to Pocatello, and because money was scarce he took a paper route at age seven and also shined shoes for a dime a pair. At nine, he started working nights in the bowling alley. He was never happy at home and often ran away with a gang of other little boys to places like Stockmen's Motor Hotel, in Elko, Nevada, where the father of one boy collared them at the slot machines and had them thrown in jail for a few hours. Another time, Bob and four or five of his friends skipped off to a desert town in Utah without any money, and Bob tried to panhandle a pedestrian who turned out to be a plainclothesman; the man bought them all breakfast and then arrested them. They were locked in a detention cell for juveniles on the top floor of the municipal building, overlooking the county courthouse, but since it was summertime the window was open, and the boys clambered up on the sill and peed on the citizens below—it was one of Bob's most vivid childhood memories.

On my first visit to Bob's condo, the place was glacially bare—the Internal Revenue Service had done a sort of spring cleaning there a few weeks earlier—but the living room was floodlit by CNN, and a big white dog, named Bear, roamed lazily around. The television noise made a cozy obbligato to Bob's talk, and every now and then his regular house guest, a man named Lynn Harris, would break in and fine-tune what Bob was saying. At home, Bob was invariably dressed in a running outfit and could have passed for a sporty suburbanite, but Lynn looked Pocatello: he wore cowboy boots and a shirt with pearl snaps and a feedlot cap, and whenever he laughed at some statement of Bob's, or merely found it unbelievable, he'd roll his head heavenward and jerk his visor down over his eyes, then flick it back up. He leaned against the mantelpiece as though it were a rail fence. He didn't talk much, but he did say that he'd known Bob since they were kids. He said he'd been a horse trader on an Indian reservation in Idaho and then had knocked about for a while in West Africa.

"Doing what?" I asked.

"Jes' nothing," he answered.

I don't know what Bob told Peg about his animal days, but I doubt whether it differed much from what he told me. He said he had left Pocatello in his mid-teens and had gone to stay with his aunt and uncle in Erlanger, Kentucky. They were sweet people who took good care of him, and whenever he could he worked odd jobs and paid them 20 percent of his earnings in exchange for bed and board. Then he went down to Florida and bought a pair of ocelots—ocelots were cheap in those days—and brought them back to Kentucky. But the ocelots died, and that made him grieve, so he bought a few more, and they also died, and he got so sick with grief, and so outraged, too, that he went down to a different Florida animal dealer, this time a reputable merchant, who explained to him about distemper shots and the care of big cats, and that got him interested in the business of buying and selling felines.

"I bought some lions from the zoo," he told me once when we were watching television, "and after that I went out and bought this beautiful leopard called Tammy and took her all over the place, including a Holiday Inn in New York, which drove the people there crazy. I never managed to get her on a TV show in New York, so I took her home. At that time I also had a poodle, who seemed to get along well with the leopard, but one day I got home and the poodle was gone. I couldn't find him anywhere, and there was no blood, no bones, no nothing but the leopard walking around with a big stomach. See, what the cat liked to do was a lot of times she would take her meat and hop in the cool bathtub and lie down and eat her steak or whatever and then lick the surface clean. It was a clean job with the poodle, too, and I couldn't really feel bad, because it wasn't like I saw him die or anything—he just kind of disappeared.

Well, I finally sold the leopard and made a really good profit: bought her for three or four hundred, sold her for thirty-five hundred or something—hey, I had to figure the poodle in there! Then I bought a pair of female lion cubs—they were wonderful—and I went out and spent five or six hundred dollars to build a nice bedroom for myself, with a stereo, in the corner of this big warehouse where the lions were going to live. One morning, though, I came in and they'd knocked down the door to my little bedroom and wrecked my chair and stereo and shredded up everything else, so I decided it was time to leave Kentucky and head out to Desert Shores, in California, where one of my friends was living, and go into the business of selling animals to rich individuals. So what I'd do was, I'd get a few ocelots and lions in—by this time I knew how to take care of them—and I'd drive them to Vegas and walk them around the casinos, and usually you'd get a guy that was half drunk, with a honey on his shoulder, and she'd go, 'Cute cat!' and I'd sell it to the guy for let's say five hundred bucks. I'd be sure to leave my phone number, because three days with an ocelot in the house is enough for most people, and I'd get it back for free. Well, one of the cats I sold got out into downtown Vegas, so they passed a special law against me that said you couldn't bring big animals into Nevada, especially not the same ones over and over."

Apparently this setback started Bob thinking. "I decided I'd go find my own animals, in Central and South America," he told me, "and I took off alone—I was about twenty-two then—and I made it as far as Nicaragua, where I became real friendly with the Somozas. Lots of people hated their guts, but I'm a warm person, and I was sitting in a restaurant behind the National Palace when I saw Luis. I knew he was the President, but I walked right over past all the bodyguards and told him who I was and shook his hand, and we started talking, and he introduced me to his right-hand man, who was called the Ear, because he went around listening to what people said about Luis. I told the Ear that I'd like not to have any more troubles with my animals at the border, and he said, 'No problem, I'll get you a gun permit and a card signed Luis Somoza, and that will make you an honorary colonel in the National Guard.' By then I was trading in ocelots, snakes, and margays that I actually toilet-trained—yep, they'd sit right up there on the toilet, though they could get a little wild, too, and destroy your whole house. I also had a spider monkey, which are nasty little guys, and some real tame jaguars—I tamed them—and pretty soon I was shipping them all by air."

Bob told me about how he wore his heart on his sleeve and would fall in love with this girl or that girl and follow her to this country or that country. He'd followed a girl to Europe and developed a taste for the Continent; then he'd sailed from Genoa to Buenos Aires and started buying and selling pre-Columbian Peruvian pottery, wood carvings, and gold artifacts. Once, he bought a big load of art for practically nothing in Peru, bribed the customs officials there, and then flew to Los Angeles and took a suitcase full of the best stuff to a gallery on La Cienega Boulevard. In the suitcase were Mochica, Nazca, and Chavín pieces, and maybe some Chimú. He didn't know what they would all fetch, but when the dealer offered him six thousand he knew they must be worth much more—

his experience in the animal business had taught him that—so they settled on nine thousand. "I'd never had that much money in my life," Bob told me, "and I just said whoop-dee-doo, that's the end of the animal business, I'm in the art business now! I didn't have to give the art distemper shots, and it wasn't going to die on me, either."

So he began to sell ancient Peruvian art to European and American art dealers, and also started exhibiting his wares at a gallery in Amsterdam owned by a dentist and connoisseur named Lou van Rijn. Bob told me that he sold to many different clients in Holland and Germany, and that he prided himself on his role in developing the German taste for pre-Columbian art. All the while, he was traveling back and forth between Europe and Buenos Aires, where he was living the high life. He drove a Porsche and had several servants, and he married a beautiful girl, the first of his six wives—though some of these marriages were really pseudo-unions, he pointed out, because you just slipped a little money to some hard-up justice of the peace for a bogus certificate to mollify the girl's parents.

"Peru was a big racket," Bob said. "In the sixties, the Peruvian government decided to register all antiquities and number them on the bottom, but they didn't take pictures of them, so people just used the same numbers over and over. 'One Nazca vase,' for Chrissake! Nowadays, they'd call you a smuggler, but it was accepted then. Everybody knew what everybody was doing."

I tried to pin Bob down about some of the people he knew, and he told me that his big problem was whether or not to trust me, but eventually he decided I was an okay sort of guy. It wasn't as if he'd never been snookered, he said. There was that time he'd transported an Easter Island head from Chile to Amsterdam, all ten tons of it, only to find out that it was fake. Once, by mistake, I asked Bob a question I had asked him the day before, and he scanned my face for an unexpressed judgment, hunted my thoughts for a secret intent. "Son-of-a-bitch is testing me," he said, flashing his character actor's smile.

Bob told me that after ten years in Argentina he decided to go to Cuiabá, in the Amazon rain forest, and try to buy some of the fine Indian spears and featherwork that he had heard were available there. He and a Swiss friend found a canoe and a guide and started working their way up the Rio Guaporé, a tributary of the Amazon, but somehow they lost all their food. They began putting in at tiny villages, whose inhabitants would feed them and give them attractive spears and blowguns or sell them vast quantities of artifacts at a discount, like the five hundred nose whistles Bob got in exchange for his inflatable mattress and later sold for a tidy sum in California. They lived in an Indian village infested with vicious flies who preyed upon them until their cheeks were drained of blood and their backs knit tight into one huge scar of bitten flesh. Bob had a .22 with him—he'd learned to shoot in Idaho and could hit a wild turkey on the run—and when he discovered that the Indians had a lot of empty Carnation cans left over from mixing up their favorite drink of evaporated milk and brackish river water, he shot a can off an Indian's head at a hundred paces, and then they all wanted so badly to

· 3 3 ·

share in the fun that he had to blast a can off every head in the village, trying to keep his cool while the tribe roared with laughter.

The day came when Bob tired of the humid jungles, as he'd tired of Nicaragua and Argentina, so he traveled up into the Peruvian Andes, where he bought himself four burros and followed the trails to remote towns and villages. There he made offers on old church paintings to the local clergy, who would cut the pictures out of their frames and roll them up for him in exchange for a modest tip. The priests, after all, were impoverished, and the canvases were falling to pieces, and Bob explained to me that if he had just left them there they'd have very soon crumbled to dust. So he loaded his burros with the Peruvian pictures—an odd assortment of devotional works—and took them back down out of the mountains and then to New Orleans, where, as luck would have it, he ran into three dames of society, and together, he told me, these women bought the pictures for the Delgado Museum (now the New Orleans Museum of Art). "And those paintings, which I think I and my partners sold for twenty thousand, are probably worth ten million by now," Bob said proudly. "So I've come up with a few winners in my life."

Peg told me she lost touch with Bob for several years in the mid-1980s; she heard from friends that he was mostly out of town. Early in 1988, though, while she was recovering from multiple fractures resulting from a freak accident in her gallery, she received a bouquet of flowers and a note from him. It appeared that Bob had married a seventeen-year-old girl named Barbara,

· 34 ·

whom he had found selling hot dogs on Monument Circle, and they now had a little boy. Peg felt too unwell to visit the family, but she renewed the old friendship by telephone, and when Bob heard that she'd been making some serious sales, he asked if she was on the lookout for anything special. As it happened, she was: a Japanese buyer with Midwestern connections had sent word that he wanted a Modigliani nude, and though no Modigliani had ever turned up in Peg's modest inventory, she thought Bob just might be able to help her find such a trophy. A few weeks later, Bob called back and told her of a painting he knew about in Holland, and despite her inability to find a listing of the piece he described in any catalogue, she considered that it might be genuine, for he mentioned a bill of sale establishing provenance. She called up the Japanese client and then her neighbor Nick Frenzel, who agreed to get Merchants National Bank, of which he was the chairman, to issue her a letter announcing the bank's intention to lend her £3 million sterling—the conditions being that the seller in Holland was willing to sell and the Japanese buyer to buy. Then, armed with a copy of a Modigliani catalogue, Peg flew off to Amsterdam. Bob, who was already in northern Europe, was to join her there.

She told me that she arrived exhausted in Amsterdam and slept for a few hours in her room at the Marriott Hotel. On rising, she threw open her window and looked out at the public gardens below, and it was as if she had seen it all before somewhere, perhaps in some photograph or at the movies: the monumental plane trees, the tidy fruit and herring stands, the weeping willows hanging over the canal, the little bridge with its fanciful ironwork spanning the green water, the copper beech ablaze in the middle distance. Across the way rose a verdigris dome and, a little to the left, a neo-Gothic gable surmounted by a peaked clock tower whose great gold numerals announced the time in this part of the world. She watched as a yellow tram crossed the bridge and eased around the bend out of sight.

Peg had never before been to Holland, yet these details teased her with their unaccountable rightness. The passersby, so many of them tall and blond, attracted her, and sensing that here for once she would not stand out in a crowd, she recalled her mother's Dutch ancestry and wondered if the notion of racial memory might contain some element of truth. It was early summer, and a soft breeze wafted the fragrance of thousands of flowers and a pungent aroma of cooking food. Her heightened taste for life was to persist throughout her stay in Amsterdam, and only much later, after the dreadful drama had reached its conclusion, did she begin to speculate about the causes of her strange exaltation—that it came, perhaps, as a too-beautiful consolation for her recent injuries and persistent pain, and also that regular doses of a powerful analgesic she was taking might have enhanced the vividness of those calamitous days.

Some hours later, Peg told me, Bob checked in at the Marriott. He informed her that the owner of the Modigliani was a Dutch antique dealer named Jack Vecht—he represented the fifth generation of Vechts in the business—whom Bob had met many years earlier during a long sojourn in Amsterdam. Then a trim, handsome, fortyish Southern Californian appeared at the hotel, and Bob introduced him as Ronald Faulk, his legal counsel, who was there to represent him in connection with the proposed purchase. This seemed odd to Peg, since she herself hadn't brought along an attorney, and anyway, Faulk's dress and manner were rather too smooth to inspire her confidence. There wasn't a wrinkle in his clothes, and she noticed with near-disbelief that his shirt cuffs and pockets were monogrammed. The three of them left the Marriott, and strolling through the streets and over five or six humpbacked bridges, they at length reached Vecht's shop, on the busy avenue known as the Rokin.

In front of the shop, a blind giant of a gypsy was working a huge street organ, but the shop itself seemed cocooned in a private stillness and silence. The green of its wooden moldings had faded almost to gray, its striped awning was glazed with dust, and the ornamental faces on the capstones over the windows had half melted into the air. The door was locked; the Americans rang; Vecht, a courtly, balding man in his seventies, wearing horn-rimmed glasses, presented himself. He showed them inside, and for a long while chatted genially with them, as if to show them that his time was all theirs. Then he informed them that the Modigliani was not in the shop—indeed, that he had no desire whatever to show it, not needing the money. Peg, meanwhile, though enjoying the figure he cut against all that lovely black delft, began to wonder whether he had ever had an expert examine the thing, and if not, why not.

At last, the merchant relented—what harm, really, could come of a peek at the picture?—and the four filed out of the shop and walked to his home on a nearby street. It was a lovely apartment, glimmering with old glassware, but when Peg caught sight of the big nude her spirits flagged, because something did not seem right about it, and when she took it down from the wall and looked it over with her magnifying glass and black light, her worst fears were confirmed. To her it felt too beautiful, too perfect—like a clever conflation of all the best features of Modigliani's work. She did not care for it, and neither Vecht's absorbing tale of how an antecedent Vecht had bought it from Modigliani himself—meeting the penniless artist at the Café du Dôme and spending a few francs for a picture he didn't particularly like—nor Bob's dismay at her fastidiousness could cause her to change her mind.

Peg was not surprised when, some hours later, Bob came around to her point of view. There was, she had begun to notice, a new ductility to the man, perhaps the result of his happy marriage to Barbara. He talked all the time about his little son, Evan, and his paternal solicitude seemed so ample that he now took Peg, too, under his protection, asking every few minutes if she was in pain or in need of a rest—she was limping noticeably. He showed her the Marriott spa, with its saunas, and they had a pleasant meal together at that old burghers' standby the Oesterbar.

Both still had business to pursue in Amsterdam—Peg, for her part, had discovered a young painter whose work she liked. The next day, while they were lunching at the hotel's sidewalk café, Bob casually mentioned that an old acquaintance was in town whom she might want to meet. This person was Michel van Rijn, the son of the van Rijn at whose gallery Bob had shown his antiquities some twenty years earlier. Bob had known Michel since Michel was a child, and remembered him as an astonishingly bright boy who had taken a liking to him and accompanied him on numerous outings. Like his father, the little Michel had been fascinated by any kind of fine workmanship, and had sometimes pestered Bob with questions as to his own worthiness to follow in his father's footsteps. He wanted to know if he, too, could learn to seek out beautiful things, if he might someday even surpass his father and become a really great dealer, one of those impresarios who introduce a whole field of overlooked objects to a delighted and grateful public. Bob had barely finished describing Michel, recounting how he had thrown himself into the field of Orthodox icons and the Christian art of the East, when the man himself appeared—a handsome fellow in an English tweed jacket, with thick dark hair and a dense mustache.

Michel at once began to tell Peg about his interest in East Christian art. She sensed in his character an appealing vulnerability, and also a certain tendency to flatter, which suggested that he was not averse to flattery himself. He was carrying a briefcase, from which he soon drew some brochures and packets of photographs and a heavy volume, edited by him, whose cover showed an icon of a melancholy saint. Michel seemed as brilliant as Bob had said he was, yet also sensitive to the impressions of others, and as he entered into a long and spirited defense of the Byzantine icon, which only in recent decades had been accepted by Western cognoscenti as a major form of expression, he would stop now and then to elicit Peg's opinion or engage her in respectful debate. Thumbing through the photographs of his current icon stock, he seemed to drift away into the half-barbaric world of ancient Byzantium, with its visions of hirsute holy men and throngs of naked martyrs huddled under gold skies, and when Peg objected to the grim subjects and stylized modes of rendering, he seemed more wounded than annoyed, and redoubled his efforts to make her sense the spirituality of these sacred treasures.

At length, and almost as an afterthought—it was one of those gestures that later seemed to have happened in a dream—he spread several pictures on the café table. They were photographs of four mosaics, two fairly whole and two in a somewhat fragile state. Of the two better-preserved mosaics, one was a roundel containing the bust of a dour-looking man with close-cropped white hair and a short beard, his head relieved against a nimbus labeled with the letters IAKOBOC; the other, also a roundel, featured a dark-haired, bearded young man with strikingly frank eyes, and bore the legend MATEOC. The third mosaic showed a figure gazing wistfully to one side, with something like a broken wing emerging from his flank, while the last one depicted a lad in his teens, who seemed to gaze up at Peg and Bob and Michel with a mild yet attentive expression.

The mosaics looked to Peg to be from the earliest Christian centuries—not so much Byzantine as Late Hellenistic; the faces seemed realistic portraits of actual people and bore some similarity to the mosaics of Sant' Apollinare Nuovo, in Ravenna. The heads weren't primitive and Oriental and unknowable, in what she then thought of as the typical Byzantine manner, but realistic and European—you could imagine them talking intelligibly to you—and the two or three whom she took to be apostles were portrayed not as insipid saints but as men of flesh and blood, thoughtful speakers and letter writers and founders of congregations. Peg's early training in the Disciples of Christ had taught her a particular respect for the apostolic faith, which is the believer's heartfelt re-enactment of the apostles' experience of Christ's teaching, and here before her lay images of some of those very men, depicted—so it seemed to her—in the days when the collective memory of their physical traits would have been almost as fresh as our memory of the faces of the Founding Fathers. Yet through her magnifying glass Peg also saw evidence of terrible decrepitude—missing tesserae, cracked plaster, menacing fissures—which tugged at her charitable nature, her susceptibility to abandoned children and wounded animals. Months later, at the trial, she would tell the court that she was "grieving" for the neglect the mosaics had been through. The figure with the broken wing (she eventually discovered that he was an archangel) seemed to speak to her with unusual poignancy, and she "fell in love"—these words, too, she would use in court—with his image and spiritual message.

Peg remembered now that a few years earlier Bob had mentioned something to her about Christian antiquities available in Europe, and she assumed that these were the pieces: Michel told her that they had been retrieved from the rubble of a church in northern Cyprus which had been destroyed during the Turkish invasion of 1974. The owner was a Turkish archaeologist who had obtained the right to buy the battered works and had transported them to his home in Munich. The archaeologist had apparently changed occupations; he had started some sort of ship-breaking business, with scrapping yards situated at various places in the Balkans, and he also dealt in antiquities, for which he had a continuing passion. The Turkish gentleman was extremely wealthy and had hitherto declined to sell the mosaics to Michel, but now his business was in trouble and he had contracted stomach or liver cancer and was undergoing radiation therapy, and the combined expenses disposed him to realize some money on the pieces. Though Michel had long wished to acquire them, he had no available funds at the moment and so would help Peg buy them instead. He guessed she could have them for about three million dollars.

Peg had never sold a piece for anywhere near that much money, and as she later told the court, she "hemorrhaged" at the mention of this price. Yet she was smitten with the mosaics, and in the next day or so, as she wandered about Amsterdam with Michel and Bob and Ronald Faulk, going to galleries and museums and a concert, they continued to discuss the pieces: who might have made them, how they had survived the depredations of the centuries, whether any museum might be interested in acquiring them, and whether, if the price should be lowered to around a million, Nick Frenzel might be persuaded to get his bank to lend her the money for a purchase. Wherever they went, people came out of shops and galleries to salute Michel; his book about East Christian art was in all the bookshops; and a poster for a show of icons he had recently organized at Delft was displayed in the windows of numerous galleries. He seemed a remarkably trusting person: for one thing, he told her the name of the wealthy Turkish gentleman, which was an unusual thing to do, since dealers rarely reveal the identity of a source; for another, he candidly informed her that he had been convicted in absentia in France for forging an artist's signature—a conviction he fiercely resented, since he certainly hadn't forged anything, he said, and hadn't even been aware that the trial was going on. He insisted to Peg, whom he now called "Peg darling," that the French practice of trying defendants in absentia was juridically abhorrent, and she concurred with this view.

It soon became clear to Peg that Ronald Faulk was not only Bob's but also Michel's legal counsel, and that if she were to buy the mosaics he would have to be involved. Neither Bob nor Michel would contribute to the price, since they both had cash-flow problems, and neither would expect a finder's commission; instead, they would settle for shares in the resale value of the pieces. And since Bob could not afford Faulk's hourly fee, it was suggested that Faulk, too, take a percentage of the resale price. Thus there would actually be five parties to any transaction—herself, the Turkish gentleman, Bob, Michel, and now this monogrammed Californian.

Peg telephoned Nick Frenzel in Indianapolis and told him that the Modigliani deal had collapsed; she also told him that she wanted to buy the mosaics. The proposal seemed to her an exercise in futility, but there was nothing to lose and Nick sounded as if he was in an expansive mood. "How much can a pile of rocks be worth?" she remembers him joking, but he also agreed to try to arrange a loan for her from Merchants Bank.

Peg now began to feel that this extraordinary coup might be possible. But how to deal with the Turk in Munich? The man was apparently dying, he didn't know her from Eve, and, as Michel pointed out, the fact that she was a woman wouldn't make matters any easier. Then Faulk offered to fly to Munich—it seemed that he had already been there on Michel's behalf a few days earlier—and he returned some hours later with a glowing description of the refinement of the Turkish gentleman, whose name was Aydin Dikmen and whose home was full of the most precious antiquities. And yes, Dikmen had agreed to sell the mosaics at a much lower price; she might even get away with half of what he had originally asked. Dikmen also seemed to have all the necessary documentation, including export licenses from Turkish Cyprus.

On July 3, 1988, Peg agreed to buy the mosaics from the Turk for a little over a million dollars. Her gallery would own them outright, with no commission paid to Bob or Michel; however, they would get half of the resale proceeds, with 5 percent of that going to Faulk for his services. Thus Bob and Michel each had a 22.5 percent stake in the merchandise. A purchase agreement was written but left unsigned, pending an examination of the pieces in Geneva (a common venue for antiquities sales, on account of the lenient Swiss banking rules and legal code); Peg was secretly hoping to bargain the Turk down once a loan of $1.2 million from Merchants Bank arrived at a corresponding bank there. Faulk was dispatched to Munich to accompany Dikmen and his treasures by air to Switzerland.

Then Peg and Bob flew to Geneva, leaving Michel behind in Amsterdam. They checked in at the Hôtel des Bergues; from her room, Peg phoned various customs offices and international agencies to see if the mosaics had been reported stolen—neglecting, however, to call any representative of either the Greek Cypriot or the Turkish Cypriot government. On July 5, she went by herself to the freehold section of the airport for a brief inspection of the pieces. Already there, standing beside four crates, was a man whom she took to be Aydin Dikmen. In later days, when the error of purchasing those mosaics filled her whole life with its enormity, her memory of the Turkish gentleman would return again and again to haunt her: a short, frail, well-dressed man, who was perspiring freely and apparently suffering from jaundice. There could be no haggling, for he did not understand English. They shook hands, and the crates were opened. She raptly inspected the mosaics. Then he motioned for the crates to be resealed, and she left. He had said nothing. She was never to see him again.

The Kanakariá mosaics had already been published, in 1977, in a volume entitled *The Church of the Panagía Kanakariá at Lythrankomí in Cyprus: Its Mosaics and Frescoes,* by A.H.S. Megaw and E.J.W. Hawkins. Megaw had been the director of antiquities for Cyprus under the British colonial administration, and Hawkins was an eminent restorer: he had cleaned the mosaics of the great Church of St. Saviour in Chora, in Istanbul. The book—one of a series of monographs sponsored by the Dumbarton Oaks Center for Byzantine Studies, in Washington, D.C., which has aided in the preservation of many Byzantine monuments—contains extensive photographs of the church, its heavily damaged frescoes, and its mosaics; the photographs were taken after completion of restoration work in the mid-1960s. The original basilica, probably built around A.D. 500, appears in the photographs as a narrow stone structure covered by a tunnel vault and surmounted by a shallow cupola, and around this edifice a later addition, consisting primarily of two side naves and a narthex, can be easily made out. There are clear close-ups of all the mosaics and frescoes. That these votive decorations had been published so recently would have suggested to an informed buyer that the appearance of any of them on the market was suspect; and this became an important issue in the trial. Cyprus claimed that Peg had known of the Dumbarton Oaks book at the time of purchase, but what she told the court, and reaffirmed to me, was that though she had been aware of the existence of some sort of publication, she had not succeeded in obtaining a copy of the monograph until six weeks after her return to the United States. Here, as with so many key episodes in the court's composite chronicle of the transaction, there was no single accepted version of the events, no story that could recommend itself as the unquestionable truth.

The mosaic cycle had decorated the apse of the church. At its heart was a geometric figure of mystical significance called a mandorla, from the Italian word for "almond." The mandorla enclosed a touchingly simple mosaic of the Blessed Virgin holding the Christ Child on her lap—an image known in Byzantine iconography as a Theotokos. Here Jesus was shown as an adolescent, not a baby, which may have been the designer's gentle reminder to the faithful that Christ was both man and God and had had to pass through all the stages of human development. On the north side of the mandorla was an archangel; his fellow on the opposite side had been missing for decades, perhaps centuries. Ten saints in roundels—there had once been twelve—graced the archivolt.

In November 1979 the Republic of Cyprus received word that although the church still stood, all its mosaics were gone. Of the ten roundels, three—Paul, Luke, and Philip—were already so fragile that they may have been destroyed in the course of removal. Two others, Jude and Bartholomew, were to resurface in the republic in 1984, under largely unexplained circumstances, and this mysterious homecoming was to become an important issue in the trial. The whereabouts of Mark, Thomas, and Andrew remained unknown. Peg Goldberg had bought Matthew and James and the North Archangel. And she had bought Christ.

Well, she had the Head of Christ, but she did not have the entire mandorla. Much of it, including the Head of Mary, had already been missing when the pieces were photographed in the 1960s; the rest had vanished either during or after the removal of the mosaics, and the strange and frightening thing was that somebody—apparently somebody shameless and brutal—had cut away the lower part, the part that showed the Hand of Mary and the Feet of Christ. This seemed an egregiously sacrilegious act, because it defiled a hallowed image, dismembering the caress with which the Mother of God, on behalf of all mankind, returns His unwavering love.

Early in the fall of 1988, after Peg had returned to Indianapolis, Michel van Rijn telephoned her from Amsterdam and announced that he had "great news." He had discovered that the Turkish gentleman also had the fragment showing the Hand and the Feet and the roundel of Saint Andrew. Michel had not yet been able to secure an option on these two pieces, but he hoped to do so soon. The thought that she possessed only some of the Kanakariá mosaics now began to disturb Peg both spiritually and aesthetically; she was also aware that partial ownership might queer an eventual sale, since sets of anything are best marketed complete. There was something irritating about the whole situation, as there always is when you buy into something and then realize that some fragment of it has been withheld and you have to go back for it. It was a little like having some part of yourself in hock, something you had to go back and *redeem*.

In the meantime, two people had bought resale shares in the mosaics. The first was an Indianapolis physician named Stewart Bick, who acquired, for a total of $780,000, half of Michel's interest and half of Bob's interest, and the second was Nick Frenzel himself, who bought 8 percent of Bick's share for an astonishing $390,000. By this time, it had begun to look as if Peg might sell the mosaics for many millions of dollars, since people all over the States were nipping, and one wealthy Greek seemed on the verge of buying. A bewildering series of loans and debt services bedeviled what had become a virtual consortium of offerers.

And then there was the sales force. By October 1988 at least four people besides Peg were trying to market the mosaics, each hoping for the giant commission. The most impressive of these would-be brokers was Geza von Habsburg, an archduke of the imperial line and a grandson of Frederick Augustus III of Saxony. An expert on Fabergé, he had served for many years as the head of Christie's European operations, and he had recently opened, with two partners, a small auction house based in Geneva and New

York. Habsburg's firm was said to stress its exceptional commitment to "discretion," and tended to favor private treaty sales, in which a potential buyer is invited to place a secret bid for the objects on offer. Habsburg proposed to arrange such a sale for the mosaics, and even agreed to advance Peg a certain amount of money, subject to proof that her title was secure. At one point, he and Peg placed a transatlantic phone call to a man purporting to be Aydin Dikmen; speaking a rudimentary German, the man sounded willing to sell them the Hand of Mary and the Feet of Christ, together with the roundel of Saint Andrew. About the same time, however, Habsburg telephoned Marion True, the antiquities curator of the J. Paul Getty Museum in Malibu, to offer the pieces to the Getty for $20 million. As it happened, Marion True enjoyed excellent relations with Dr. Vassos Karageorghis, the director of the Greek Cypriot Department of Antiquities, and warning Habsburg of possible flaws in the seller's title to the mosaics, she notified Cyprus that four Early Christian works had suspiciously appeared on the market.

All this time, Peg's infatuation with the North Archangel was growing. She even thought for a while that she might not sell him at all but keep him for herself. "He gave off such an aura—it was like white light," she told me later, when, rather against my will, I'd become fascinated with the mosaics case and was trying to figure out what had happened to her. "I had this strange déjà vu—it was like I'd always known him, yet hadn't. I had recurring dreams of knowing him—of knowing who he was. The day I finally got hold of the Dumbarton Oaks monograph on the mosaics, I opened it and realized that for several days I'd been humming that old song from the fifties—'Got an angel on my shoulder.' I hadn't thought about that song since I was a kid."

By late autumn Peg's phone conversations with Michel van Rijn had gone sour. According to Peg, he sounded possessive about the mosaics and disdainful of her selling techniques, and he was trying to wheedle her into changing the terms of the deal so that he would have a larger resale share and sole control of the marketing. "Peg darling, it's not right, it's not fair," he would say, over and over, and the next thing she knew he swam into her dreams, with his thick mustache and breathy Dutch accent. "I just couldn't escape his influence," she told me. "He was inside my head. I had nightmares. It was like some sort of possession. Part of me just wanted to escape him, but part of me—the social worker in me—wanted to help him. I guess I was trying to help Bob, too. Do you know that movie *Pretty Woman,* where Julia Roberts keeps saying, 'Bad mistake'? Well, that was it for me, too. *Bad* mistake. *Bad* judge of character."

Early that winter, Michel called to announce that he had finally persuaded the Turkish gentleman to sell the Hand and Feet plus Andrew. On February 10, 1989, a new purchase agreement was signed by Peg, Bob, Michel, and Stewart Bick allowing them, by exercise of Michel's new option, to buy these items; but by this time the Embassy of Cyprus was already taking steps, and the mosaics were never reunited.

The removal of the mosaics from the Kanakariá church could not have taken place without the partition of Cyprus in 1974. It has been a long time since the Greeks and Turks of Cyprus have agreed on much of anything, and they do not agree, to say the least, on what brought about the Turkish invasion in the summer of that year, the Turks claiming that Ankara intervened, in accordance with the 1960 Treaty of Guarantee, to protect the Turkish minority from persecution, and the Greeks insisting that the invasion was part of an irredentist design. Whatever the case, the island had already been partitioned a decade earlier, de facto, by the withdrawal of much of the Turkish population into defended enclaves and by the Cypriot republic's imposition of an economic blockade on these enclaves, one of which occupied much of Nicosia, the capital. When the invasion came, it drove more than 200,000 Greek Cypriots from their homes and left 37 percent of the island in Turkish hands. The so-called Green Line has divided the two communities ever since, with the Greeks living in the south and the Turks in the north, and a United Nations force stationed between the two. The south continued to be called the Republic of Cyprus and to regard itself as the sole legitimate authority over the entire island, while the north decided to style itself the Turkish Federated State of Cyprus, changing its name a few years later to the Turkish Republic of Northern Cyprus. This ministate has remained heavily dependent on Turkey and is garrisoned by Turkish troops.

During and after the invasion, the cultural property of both communities suffered considerable damage, but the Greeks were especially grieved by their losses. They had a lot more to lose—the island's Greek treasures by far outnumbered its Turkish ones—and they had also been forced to give up large tracts of territory inhabited mostly by Greeks. Cyprus has an unusually dense concentration of important Byzantine monuments, and the looting of these buildings was particularly widespread—irreparable damage was done to the Antiphonitis Monastery, to the church of St. Themonianos, outside the village of Lysi, and to many other Orthodox Christian precincts in the north—which suggested to the Greeks that the Turks were pursuing a policy of anti-Greek vandalism. This theory has been disputed by some authoritative outside observers, who note the Turks' relative impoverishment and their eagerness to build a tourist industry oriented toward countries whose populations profess Christianity; yet the destruction of churches and the theft or defacement of icons was a painful reality all the same. In some cases, Turkish troops from the mainland probably indulged in opportunistic pillage; in others, soldiers or local ruffians casually vandalized any visible symbol of the hated enemy. More ominously, signs appeared that a sophisticated international smuggling ring was operating with near-impunity; Turkish journalists reported instances in which the ring had bribed minor officials. UN soldiers regularly crossed the Green Line, and a few senior officers seem to have been corrupted with remarkable ease; some female couriers are thought to have availed themselves of the traditional Turkish reluctance to search women. Because no country but Turkey extended diplomatic recognition to the Turkish Republic of Northern Cyprus, outside funding for the maintenance and protection of the antiquities there was unavailable. Hundreds of icons, in fresco, mosaic, or paint on panel, vanished from the island, and their disappearance opened a terrible wound in the Greek Cypriot soul.

One reason is that these pictures have been regarded for almost two millennia as the traditional vehicles of contact with the Almighty. Though the worship of icons is not direct but "honorific," or "relative"—you pray not to the icon itself but to what it depicts—an image of a sacred personage, such as the Blessed Virgin, is not just a symbol; it actively partakes of her nature if made with the requisite purity and cherished in the correct way. In popular Orthodoxy, icons function a little like relics, and some of them actually are. Jesus was thought to have impressed His features on a cloth and sent it to King Abgar of Edessa, where it was long venerated; if a holy man touched something, and then you touched the same thing, he touched you—there were edible icons, made out of hardened bits of earth from the Miraculous Mountain of St. Simeon Stylites. For simple, devout people, icons have supernatural powers: they weep, bleed, guarantee contracts, speak on occasion, move across water without getting wet, cure ailments, and if carried about the walls of a besieged city protect it from infidel armies. Size and artistic merit are irrelevant to sanctity, and the millions of tiny, commercially manufactured portraits strewn throughout the Orthodox world are all devotionally equidistant from the Pantocrator and His saints.

The Kanakariá mosaics are not only votive objects, however. They are also a prime part of the heritage of modern Cyprus, the tiny nation born in 1960; the icons of Cyprus were being catalogued for the first time when Turkish troops invaded in 1974. The treasures of Cypriot craftsmanship are seen as the islanders' invaluable patrimony, part of what spiritually defines them, and the loss of any major Cypriot work of art is experienced as deeply painful. The soul of a people, even a very small people, is inevitably furnished with memories of material things—of mountains and rivers and cities and shrines—and the appearance of an unmistakably Cypriot angel on the shoulder of some lady in Indianapolis was not something that either the Church or the Republic of Cyprus could tolerate. Cyprus filed suit for a recovery action in federal court in Indianapolis on March 29, 1989.

2

Peg now had to find some very good lawyers. She turned for help to her banker friend Nick Frenzel, who recommended hiring Baker & Daniels, the oldest law firm in Indiana and one of the best. He also suggested that she press for a relatively brief "discovery period"—the period set aside for the gathering and disclosure of facts and documents—so that their meter might not run for too long; he pointed out that unless she could pay off her debt to Merchants Bank she'd better put a cap on her legal expenses. Counsel for the defendant would be Joe Emerson, a brilliant, mild-mannered expert in corporate litigation on the federal-court level, while Cyprus's chief attorney would be Thomas Kline, of the Washington, D.C., firm of Manatt, Phelps, Rothenberg, & Phillips, who specialized in environmental and antitrust law. Neither had ever tried an antiquities case, but both were eager to take on a lawsuit of historic importance.

During the two months scheduled for discovery, the opposing legal teams took more than twenty depositions. Neither Kline nor Emerson knew much about Cyprus or the issue of national cultural patrimony, and most of the time they were at a disadvantage. Some of the deponents were extremely evasive and gave barely credible testimony; together they wove a tapestry of whispers, hints, clues, hole-and-corner confidences, and taunting equivocations, so that today when you read their statements at a stretch—or, rather, when you read *in* them, for piled up they stand six feet off the floor—you get the eerie feeling of entering a far-flung delusional system, a sort of *folie à tous*. The antiquities world evidently counted many players in many countries and in several tiers. Some were clearly illicit traffickers; others maintained a façade of gentility but weren't averse to dealing with traffickers; and others turned their backs on the traffickers—or, at least, made it look that way. People cut themselves into several deals in a single day, cruising about with their portable phones, so that in time the story of Peg's purchase came to seem only one chapter in a vast *Arabian Nights* of interrelated mercantile episodes. The mountain of testimony did not solve a mystery so much as spawn one.

In the welter of dubious persons and documents, the Turkish gentleman seemed particularly fishy—his name was spelled "Dikmen," "Dikman," or "Diekman," and his signature varied a lot. Kline began to wonder if maybe he wasn't someone of a different name altogether, or perhaps several people, or an Anatolian tribe, or nobody at all. Almost from the start, Kline impressed upon his colleagues the importance of assuming that there was no Aydin Dikmen unless some evidence to the contrary should be presented. They would only be frustrated by the attempt to clarify uncertainties they didn't need to have clear. Who had the better title, Cyprus or Peg? That was the decisive question. Kline had a lot of experience as a litigator; he'd taken his knocks, he'd examined many different kinds of witnesses, and he was not going to be thrown off his stride by these funny art people— certainly not by someone like Bob Fitzgerald, who kept all his records in a midden in his garage and was reported to have gone by several different names.

One of Kline's chief headaches was that he couldn't be certain whether Indiana law or Swiss law would be found to apply, since Switzerland, after all, had been the place of purchase. In Indiana, a purchaser cannot receive good title from a thief, whereas under Swiss law a good-faith purchaser may acquire good title to stolen articles five years after the theft. Kline held that the transaction had only a fleeting connection to Switzerland, and that Indiana law should govern the issues in this case. Under Indiana law, Peg would have trouble claiming good title to the pieces, since, Kline would argue, the Church of Cyprus had never given or sold them to anybody.

As is common in litigation, however, Kline also staked out the alternative, or contingent, position. Suppose Swiss law should be found to apply—what then? He maintained that under the application of Swiss law Peg did not qualify as a good-faith purchaser—that suspicious circumstances should have caused her to question whether the seller could convey good title. There was the peculiar nature of the intermediaries, Fitzgerald, van Rijn, and Faulk; the baffling obscurity of the export papers, which, he noted, she didn't actually see until some months after the purchase; the fact that the art had been published by Dumbarton Oaks only a decade before; and her failure to produce evidence of her alleged search for reports of theft. The defendant "claims she fell in love with the mosaics at a glance," Kline said in his pre-trial brief. "However, she does not want them for what they are or convey so beautifully, even after fourteen centuries; she wants the opportunity to profit—enormously—from the plunder of others."

Joe Emerson, defending Peg against Kline's two-tiered strategy, turned out to be a litigator who could argue very cogently on paper but was rather less effective in court. (During the trial, a reporter noticed that Emerson could not at first pronounce "Sotheby's," and he often found himself in the unenviable position of having to ask questions to which he could not even guess the answers. He told me that he had at times been unnerved by the barrage of devious and misleading statements to which he was continually subjected by witnesses.) In his brief, Emerson naturally claimed that Swiss law governed the issue of Peg's title, and that both her inquiries and her purchase had been made in good faith. He noted her levelheadedness in July 1988, as demonstrated by her refusal to buy the Modigliani. He reminded the court that she had made phone calls to customs officials and to established centers of information on art theft; that she had obtained an appraisal of the mosaics not only from Michel van Rijn but also from two specialists; and that she had procured what she reasonably believed to be valid export documents. As for the trustworthiness of Michel van Rijn and Bob Fitzgerald, they were mere finders, not the seller himself, and in any event, Peg wasn't buying Fitzgerald and van Rijn, she was buying the mosaics.

As Emerson proceeded to collect evidence, he began to see that the weakest aspect of Cyprus's case was the long period between the discovery that the mosaics were missing and the demand for the return of the property. Under Indiana law, a victim of theft who demonstrably knows or suspects the identity of the thief and fails to take action against him may have a very hard time suing the purchaser of the stolen goods. Moreover, when victims of theft "sleep on their rights," it may be a sign that their hands are not clean. What Indiana wags were now calling the "gaps in the apse" had first been reported to the Cypriot government in 1979, but that government had not demanded the return of the mosaics until almost ten years later. Emerson argued that Cyprus had had ample reason to suspect that Aydin Dikmen had the mosaics—a suspicion that should have arisen at least by 1982, when the Turkish Cypriot newspaper *Ortam*, which the Greek Cypriots monitored, published an article connecting Dikmen with the theft of Christian art from a castle in Kyrenia, a port in northern Cyprus. (A photo of the stolen Kanakariá mosaics appeared at the top of the page, though their theft was not attributed to Dikmen.) At the time, Dikmen was operating quite openly in Munich, giving his name and address on his bills of sale and listing his number in the Munich telephone directory. It was strange, if not damning, that Cyprus had failed to put a detective on the case, to notify Interpol, to alert the customs service of any nation, or to proceed against Dikmen under the available provisions of West German law.

A key figure for Kline was Constantine Leventis, the Republic of Cyprus's ambassador to UNESCO. In a deposition taken by Joe Emerson a week before the trial, he testified that Cyprus had put out word of the disappearance of the Kanakariá mosaics just months after the theft was reported in 1979. A small, modest, rather straitlaced man in his mid-forties, Leventis had inherited a vast fortune and become a respected philanthropist; he was the director of the Leventis Foundation, which funded socially useful projects in Cyprus and West Africa. Though he claimed to have only a slight interest in art, noting that he had no art collection save for "a few watercolors," he was privy to a lot of information about objects already recovered by Cyprus. When Emerson questioned him about the circumstances surrounding that strange reappearance in 1984 of two of the mosaics (the roundels depicting Jude and Bartholemew), Leventis replied that they had been returned to Cyprus, along with two fakes, through the agency of a London art dealer named Yanni Petsopoulos, who had arranged for them to be left in a warehouse in Frankfurt for the Cypriot Embassy people in Bonn to pick up. Had Leventis known the name of the man who had been in possession of them? Emerson asked. No, he had not, and so far as he was aware, neither had anyone in the Greek Cypriot government or the Church of Cyprus.

As Emerson went about gathering evidence, *The Indianapolis Star* ran an astonishing interview with an out-of-state museum expert on the significance of the forthcoming trial. This was Walter Hopps, the curator of contemporary art at the Menil Collection in Houston, and he went on at such length that Peg called Joe Emerson and said, "Joe, that man's hiding something—subpoena him." Emerson thereupon obtained a court order to depose Hopps and his employer, Dominique de Menil.

Mrs. de Menil, née Schlumberger, who owned enormous amounts of Schlumberger stock left to her by her father and uncle, was then almost eighty years old; she had founded the Menil Collection, a museum based on her own holdings and named after her late husband, John de Menil, about ten years earlier. Rather preachily high-minded, and long fascinated by the spiritual side of art, she had fallen in love with Eastern Orthodox culture and amassed one of the finest Byzantine collections in the country. Nobody expected to see her name dragged into a lawsuit involving smuggling and theft; nobody expected to see her expense records subpoenaed along with those of people who spelled "Cyprus" as "Cypress" or offered forms printed in German as Turkish state documents.

Mrs. de Menil's deposition was taken in Houston. What her testimony revealed was that the Menil Foundation (the parent of the collection) had, like Peg, bought Cypriot antiquities from the Turkish gentleman, and that the Cypriot government had been well aware of it, for the very simple reason that Mrs. de Menil had ransomed the antiquities back on their behalf.

What had happened was this: In June 1983, Yanni Petsopoulos—a polished and highly articulate carpet and icon merchant who came from a wealthy Constantinopolitan publishing family—told Walter Hopps and Mrs. de Menil that he had discovered two Byzantine frescoes, cut up into segments, in the possession of a Turkish businessman who lived in an apartment in Munich. He took his two clients there, and the Turk showed them a drawing of the ruined basilica from which the frescoes had supposedly been removed; he said he had uncovered this building near a town in Anatolia while bulldozing a site for a new youth hostel. He also showed them photographs of the frescoes, and several individual fragments. But they doubted the Turkish provenance and soon established that the paintings were in fact from the tiny church of St. Themonianos, near Lysi, in Turkish Cyprus. They then got in touch with Dr. Karageorghis, the Greek Cypriot antiquities director, who after lengthy negotiations managed to persuade His Beatitude Archbishop Chrysostomos of the Church of Cyprus to let the Menil Collection buy the frescoes, restore them, and mount them in a specially built chapel in Houston for fifteen years, after which they would be returned to the Church of Cyprus.

These revelations composed a dark and dramatic tale of the rescue of vanished works of art, but the problem for Cyprus was that they also suggested that the republic's officials had already had dealings with Dikmen, and had thus arguably compromised their recovery action against Peg.

Walter Hopps, in his deposition, offered further revelations that put Cyprus in an even more difficult position. He testified that shortly after his visit to Dikmen's apartment with Mrs. de Menil, Petsopoulos said that he'd noticed a mosaic roundel of a saint's head hanging on a wall over a certain red sofa. "I wonder if it isn't a piece of the Kanakariá mosaics," Petsopoulos had remarked. Hopps asked, "What are the Kanakariá mosaics?" And Petsopoulos exclaimed, "Haven't you ever seen? You don't know?"

Hopps went on to disclose that in 1985 or 1986 he visited Cyprus and saw the two roundels recovered by the Church in 1984, and that neither of them was the one he and Petsopoulos had seen hanging over Dikmen's sofa. Since the Dumbarton Oaks monograph showed that at least nine of the Kanakariá mosaics were in fair condition before the Turkish invasion, and since Cyprus had two and Dikmen apparently had one, six were still missing in 1986. And the obvious question was: If Dikmen had one, wasn't it a pretty good guess that he also had the six others? His phone number and address were right there in the Munich telephone directory, as Emerson kept on repeating, yet the Cypriot government had never gone after him.

And that was where the remarkable part of Hopps's testimony came in. He recounted the negotiations with the Cypriots over the Lysi frescoes, and how Dr. Karageorghis had demanded of him, "I must ask you in whose hands these frescoes are at present," and how he had absolutely refused to answer, citing a warning from Petsopoulos that the possessor might destroy the frescoes or seek vengeance on somebody if he should come to feel hunted. Emerson was skeptical of this conversation as Hopps described it; when he questioned Hopps closely on whether he had any evidence that Dikmen had ever done or could do such a destructive thing, Hopps said no, he did not. Nevertheless, the Menil Foundation, like one acceding to extortion or kidnapping, had declined to reveal Dikmen's name to the Cypriot authorities; and the truly providential thing was that Yanni Petsopoulos had never revealed it, either.

According to Hopps, it was Petsopoulos who had persuaded the Turkish gentleman to return, absolutely free of charge, the two Kanakariá mosaics that

turned up in Cyprus in 1984. And between Petsopoulos and Dikmen, Hopps said, there had been an
"enormous emotional explosion" over Dikmen's con-
cealment of the true origin of the Lysi frescoes. It was
here that the story became lurid, Oriental: At Dikmen's villa outside the Turkish city of Konya, Petsopoulos had dinner with Dikmen and his family, and
then, when the two men retired to Dikmen's study—
this was Hopps's version—Petsopoulos "picked up a
decanter, hurled and smashed it against the wall in
the fireplace, to sort of punctuate what he was going
to say next, and then shouted, 'How could you have
lied to us?' " And then Dikmen—the same man whom
Petsopoulos had represented to Hopps, and Hopps
had represented to Karageorghis, as a possibly ruthless felon—came meekly to the conclusion that "the
honorable thing to do was to turn over what he had
of the mosaics." No money changed hands, and neither Karageorghis nor Constantine Leventis had occasion to learn the name of the man who had
disgorged these fragments of the Cypriot patrimony.
    Much later, Petsopoulos would claim, to me, that
Hopps's memory had failed him on certain minor
points. But such, at all events, was Hopps's extraordinary testimony; to some it seemed as if God Himself had ordained through all the labyrinthine turnings
of this affair that the name of Aydin Dikmen should
never fall upon the ears of any representative of the
Republic of Cyprus. Peg gave Hopps's story no credence, but to her outrage, nobody would stand up
and swear that he was wrong, and so it was duly
entered into evidence and accepted without demurral
by the court. Within hours of testifying, Hopps resigned his position at the Menil Collection.

It was during the taking of Peg's own deposition, in late April and early May, mostly in the offices of a legal reporting service in downtown Indianapolis, that she got her first look at Tom Kline. He turned out to be a smallish, scholarly-looking man in horn-rimmed glasses who did nothing to improve her opinion of attorneys. Seemingly baffled by the many commercial documents she'd submitted in evidence, he betrayed all too clearly his desire to sidestep a confrontation with her. Yet underneath, like most lawyers, he was obviously an assumer, and what he assumed, she thought she detected, was that this Midwestern lady art dealer had got in over her head and was too inexperienced even to know it. He also had the lawyer's booby-trapped politeness, so that even his self-restraint, his way of never interrupting or pressuring her, felt like a sly sort of trick. She had, however, come fully armed—in business attire, and with Joe Emerson and another lawyer by her side— and she noted with satisfaction that Kline as he questioned her was obliged to watch the notary type the long list of her academic honors and the longer record of her public service into the deposition transcript. When at length Kline started quizzing her about her purchase of the disputed mosaics, she felt perfectly in control of the dialogue. Firm and composed, maybe even a little stern, she thought she could perceive what he wanted and granted him no leeway to misconstrue her motives.

Several weeks later the proceedings resumed, and this time Peg didn't bother to wear a business outfit. She came in a sweatshirt-style top slashed with bold bars of color, ready to spar more frankly with Kline yet also confident that she would be vindicated. In a way, his questioning could help her—help her to tell her side of the story.

She noticed that he had brought along a heavily marked-up calendar, and presently he asked her when she'd first learned that the mosaics had been published. She replied that Michel had informed her of this.

"Informed you about the Dumbarton Oaks publication?" Kline asked bluntly.

"Oh, no," she countered.

"What *did* he tell you about?"

"That they were published in some letter, like a journal."

Kline made a note of her reply. Then he asked, "When did you first learn about the Dumbarton Oaks publication?"

"Several weeks after my return to the United States," she answered, somewhat annoyed at his probing. What this lawyer treated as a board game was her one-and-only life, but she decided not to betray her irritation.

Further along Kline asked her where she understood that Dikmen had found the mosaics. She said, "I believe I was informed that he had found them in the rubble of the interior of the church, and had removed them."

"Do you recall whether it was Mr. van Rijn who made that statement?" he asked.

"Yes, it was," she conceded, rather testily. Kline had the litigator's way of dealing himself a card.

"At that time," he went on, "did either Mr. van Rijn or Mr. Fitzgerald say anything else about where Mr. Dikmen had gotten those mosaics from, or how he had gotten them?"

"That he was an archaeologist by education," she said. "That he had received an undergraduate degree from one of the universities in Turkey, and that his graduate degree was from one of the—I guess I would call them 'Eastern' countries. That he had at least one book in progress at that time. That he had been the official archaeologist for the northern portion of Cyprus, and I believe he had held a position with the Turkish government for various types of archaeological excavation in Turkey."

"Most of this information about Dikmen's credentials came from Mr. van Rijn?" Kline asked.

"I believe that's correct," she answered. "It's also possible that it came from Mr. Faulk."

From *Faulk*? Kline looked at her with renewed curiosity, then asked her, in his usual unforced manner, "Do you know whether Mr. Faulk had met Mr. Dikmen previously?"

She thought for a moment. "I'm under the impression that he had," she replied.

That interested him; in fact, he seemed extremely interested in the growing importance of Faulk to the whole case. He asked her what other business Faulk had taken in hand, and she told him that she had asked the Californian to assist her in all negotiations.

"You felt more comfortable turning to Mr. Faulk because he was an attorney?" Kline suggested. "Even though you had known Mr. Fitzgerald for some time and had just met Mr. Faulk?"

"That's correct," she replied.

Kline couldn't conceal his professional amazement. Faulk, after all, was van Rijn's and Fitzgerald's lawyer, whereas she had her own attorney back in Indianapolis, a man named Ezra Friedlander, who handled her gallery's routine legal matters. "Is there any reason," Kline said, "why you did not consider bringing Mr. Friedlander over to assist you?"

"Actually I did—at a later point."

"When did he come over?"

"I did *consider*."

"Oh, you did *consider* at a later point. I see."

When, a few hours later, the proceedings finally ended, Peg felt that she'd acquitted herself reasonably well. She had stuck to her guns: there was no doubt that the enemy respected her.

The trial itself began in federal court in Indianapolis in late May 1989. The judge was James E. Noland, an elderly Democrat of solid reputation. Father Maheriotis testified on behalf of the Church of Cyprus, and two learned international-law experts testified, and so did several Cypriot officials and a former caretaker of the church in Lythrankomí. Michel van Rijn was not asked by either side to testify: Emerson took note of his quarrel with Peg, whereas Kline felt that his presence might elicit a certain sympathy for her.

The most withering of the plaintiffs' expert witnesses turned out to be Gary Vikan, the curator of medieval art at the Walters Art Gallery, in Baltimore, who was eloquent, wry, and conversant with all manner of Byzantine lore. Vikan wearily spelled out "provenance" for the court stenographer and made coolly cutting remarks about art dealers—including Michel van Rijn, about whom, strangely enough, he seemed to know something.

It was during Vikan's testimony that the courtroom assembly—packed as it was with Cypriots, Greek-

American students, law-review commentators, and museum attorneys—began to display signs of leaning toward the plaintiffs. Whenever Vikan spoke there was absolute silence; whenever he finished there was a murmur of approval. Toward the end of his testimony, Kline asked him what he would have done if he had been offered this deal, and he replied, "Walked."

Despite Vikan's performance, however, Emerson believed that Kline had failed to prove the Cypriots' diligence in trying to regain the mosaics, for presently he rose to move for dismissal of the lawsuit. The evidence was all in Exhibit 314, he said, holding up that telltale copy of *Ortam* with its story about the Kyrenia Castle robbery. "This was the Turkish news article that had the picture of the Kanakariá mosaics at the top and the name of Aydin Dikmen in the headline," Emerson reminded the court. "Cyprus also knew that the Kanakariá mosaics were located in Munich, Germany. Now, Your Honor, if there ever was a clear case of sitting on your rights and not pursuing your rights, this is such a case." But His Honor did not agree, and the trial went forward.

Bob Fitzgerald was called to the witness stand, by Kline, on the morning of June 2. He had come to the courthouse in elegant attire, which for him was unusual, and accompanied by his beautiful young wife. He was observed staring covetously at Father Maheriotis's gold-crested pastoral staff, as if he contemplated making the abbot an offer for it. To some in the courtroom his manner seemed debonair; to his friend Peg it was infuriatingly flippant. When asked to read one of the exhibits, he casually disclosed that he had forgotten to bring his glasses.

After questioning Bob on the circumstances of the sale, Kline said something that made the courtroom buzz: he asked if it was true that Michel van Rijn had paid Aydin Dikmen only $350,000 for the mosaics. This figure was about a third of what Peg had shelled out; but during the discovery process Ronald Faulk had produced a secret purchase agreement—a contract among the three middlemen—showing this sum. It was obvious that a very large piece of change—something like $750,000—had never reached the pockets of Aydin Dikmen, assuming that such a person existed. Faulk's deposition stated that he himself, on the side, had received $80,000 of this as compensation for his services, but that still left roughly $650,000 unaccounted for.

"Where did the $650,000 go?" Kline asked Bob.

"Seventy thousand of it went to an attorney in London," Bob replied.

"This was your attorney?"

"Michel van Rijn's attorney and my attorney."

"So the two of you took seventy for an attorney?"

"Approximately seventy. It would have been seventy-one or seventy-two."

"That leaves $580,000, if my arithmetic is still holding. Where did the $580,000 go?"

"That was divided between Michel and myself."

Suddenly the picture was clear. For a few hours of sweet-talking Peg Goldberg in Amsterdam, Fitzgerald and van Rijn had netted $580,000 for brokering the four mosaics, and this sum was in addition to their subsequent earnings on the sale to Stewart Bick of their back-end interests in the pieces.

A few minutes later, Jay Yeager, Emerson's young associate, rose to cross-examine Bob. It was an errand of mercy for Peg. Was Peg aware, he asked, of how little money was really going to Dikmen?

"She didn't know," said Bob.

"Did you ever discuss with her the amount, at any time?" Yeager asked.

"I did not."

"Before the transaction?"

"I did not."

"Did she ask you about it?"

"Yes."

"She asked you about it more than once?"

"Several times."

"Why didn't you tell her, Mr. Fitzgerald?" Yeager asked.

"Because I told her it wasn't any of her business," said Bob.

Peg remembered no such candor on Bob's part, and she later told me that she wanted to reach across and pound Bob's head on the table. She was also beginning to understand how much information had been withheld from her, and that this trial was not the end but the beginning of an adventure.

Not until the penultimate day of the trial did Peg take the stand in her own defense, to be questioned first by Emerson and then, in cross-examination, by Kline. Emerson was by now quite concerned to portray Michel as a reputable dealer—or at least as a dealer who'd seemed so to Peg—and he asked her what impression van Rijn had made on her. "I really liked him," she answered. "He was personable. He was very intelligent, very articulate, very well-read. We had a great time talking about many things."

Then, to burnish Michel's image, Emerson said, "What does 'van Rijn' mean in Dutch, or what is it?"

"I asked him if he was descended from Rembrandt," she replied, "and he indicated that he was, and also that his mother's side of the family is Rubens."

"Did he appear knowledgeable in matters of Byzantine art?"

"Yes, very much so, because he was very upset that I was castigating some of the things that he perceived as treasures."

Then came Kline's turn. Though theoretically it wasn't necessary for him to prove that Peg had made a bad-faith purchase, much was actually riding on that issue, for Judge Noland had announced his intention of at least considering the case in the light of Swiss law. Eleven months earlier, Peg had stood before a great decision, to buy or not to buy, and nothing would be more revealing now than a close look at her inquiries, her caution, her scruples—or the lack of them.

Until now, Kline had spent much of his courtroom life arguing antitrust and environmental cases to largely empty halls, where experts confabbed in whispers and clerks studied their shoes; this was different. These crowds, these cameras, this suspense—this was like a full-dress trial on television. He knew about "Hoosier hospitality" and felt that Judge Noland was extending it to him, so he resolved to avoid quibbles with opposing counsel, slurs on the defendant, anything that the court might construe as a cannonade. Now, in his most important cross-examination, he carefully reviewed the events leading up to the sale: the tip about the Modigliani, the bank's astonishing letter, the plane flight to Holland, the arrival of Bob, the appearance of Ronald Faulk and Michel van Rijn, the first serious discussion of the mosaics. Painting the picture he needed, he placed the middlemen very close to one another, in suspiciously cozy attitudes; they formed a closed circle of cronies, which Peg had never tried to break out of. He wished, as he later put it to me, "to highlight the suggestion that she was aware of a setup."

"Now, I'm correct, am I not," he asked her, "that Mr. Fitzgerald mentioned the mosaics over lunch in Amsterdam?" She replied that this was so, and they discussed the lunch a little further. Then Kline asked her, "Didn't Mr. Fitzgerald indicate to you, before Mr. van Rijn joined the conversation, that he had previously told Mr. van Rijn about you and that you might be interested in these mosaics?"

"In a general sort of way, yes," she answered.

"I'm not sure I understand what that means," Kline said. "Did he or did he not tell you that he had indicated to Mr. van Rijn who you were and that you might be interested in the mosaics?"

"Yes," she replied.

"Now, at some point Mr. van Rijn joined you during the conversation and Mr. Fitzgerald introduced you to him?"

"That's correct."

"You had not known Mr. van Rijn previously?"

"No."

"And at some point Mr. Fitzgerald told you that Mr. van Rijn was a published author?"

"Yes."

Kline suggested that Michel's book, *Icons and East Christian Art,* was merely a vanity publication, and she was obliged, somewhat uncomfortably, to concur. He asked her if she had known of Michel's little contretemps with the French courts; yes, she admitted, she had.

Kline then turned to Ronald Faulk's appearance in Amsterdam. Had Bob told her that Faulk was there to represent him in connection with the Modigliani and other matters? She answered yes, that he had.

"During this conversation, you developed the impression that Mr. Faulk had already been to see Mr. Dikmen, didn't you?" Kline asked.

"I'm not sure," she replied, hedging. "I believe so."

Then Kline went on to Peg's contention that she had, at the time, accepted Michel as a reliable expert on East Christian art. "Now, Miss Goldberg," he said, "this morning I believe you testified that Mr. van Rijn told you the mosaics were either fourth- or fifth-century mosaics, and at your deposition I believe you said that he told you they were late fifth-century. Do you recall exactly what Mr. van Rijn told you about the age of the mosaics?"

"I remember that we had a series of discussions, because I thought that they were earlier than he suggested, and we were discussing it back and forth," she said.

"That is consistent with my memory of your deposition," Kline granted. "He thought that—he told you he thought they were from the late fifth century. But you knew better, didn't you?"

"I thought better," she said, falling into the trap. She stood ready to defend her critical acumen, but Kline had already scored his point. Soon Peg granted that Michel, whom she had claimed to be "very knowledgeable," had also misidentified two of the pieces.

Then Kline turned to the question of Dikmen's

identity. He asked, "Either Mr. van Rijn or Mr. Faulk told you that Mr. Dikmen was a published archaeologist, and that in addition to having been the official archaeologist for the northern portion of Cyprus, he had also held a position with the Turkish government for various types of archaeological excavations in Turkey, is that correct?"

"I can't remember exactly when I found out that he was a published archaeologist," she answered, "but that he had been an archaeologist in both roles, yes."

"You never saw anything that had been published by Mr. Dikmen as an archaeologist?" he asked.

"No."

"And you never saw any document indicating he was the official archaeologist for the so-called Turkish Federated State of Cyprus?"

"I didn't personally see it, but Mr. Faulk indicated he had seen the document." *Faulk* again.

By now it was apparent to careful spectators that Kline had a keen insight into human nature. Though he conceivably nursed a truant sympathy for Peg, who had obviously bought more than she bargained for, something about her bothered him. Perhaps it was the manner in which she had brazened her way through the perilous moments in her deposition—what he saw as her weird resistance to awakening fully to her predicament. She was overconfident, and he evidently figured that he might be able to draw her out with sops to her self-regard.

He said, "Miss Goldberg, one of the questions you had early on about the mosaics, besides whether they were fake, was the notion of whether someone else might consider them to be stolen property, isn't that correct?"

"Whether there were any reports of them being missing and stolen, that's correct," she answered.

"I'm asking a different question," Kline said. "My question is whether you had a concern that someone might consider them to be stolen property."

It fell to her now to express a passionate sympathy for the victims of theft, but instead she raised a technical point. "No," she said. "My concern was whether or not they had ever been *reported* missing or stolen."

"And how do you understand that to be different?" Kline asked.

"Because it is semantically different," she answered.

"Explain to me in *content* how it is different," he requested.

"Well, it is one thing to check with—to go through a list of checking appropriate agencies and discussing with the officials whether there is any report that anything has ever been reported stolen or missing, and it is another thing for someone to come out of the woodwork and say, 'By the way, that is mine.' I mean, those are two different things."

She had wandered into a verbal bog, and he at once rephrased his question. "When you set out to make these phone calls," he said, "it was your purpose only to determine whether some claim had already been registered somewhere with these agencies about these mosaics, is that correct?"

"And whether there was an applicable treaty" came her unguarded reply.

"You were not trying to determine whether there was someone out there who might consider these to be stolen property?"

"I think I have already answered that."

"Well, indulge me and answer it again," he insisted. "That was not what you were trying to do?"

"Well, if there were someone out there who regarded them as stolen property, I would expect that, with the agencies I contacted, the name of the person or organization or country would have been revealed."

"And it was for that reason that you determined that the only inquiry you were going to make was to see whether these mosaics had ever been *registered* somewhere as stolen or missing, is that correct?"

"I don't think you are classifying it properly," she objected.

So it went for a while, thrust and parry, until Kline asked, "So, you never called Cyprus?" Suddenly his voice sounded tense.

"I called the government—I called northern Cyprus. I mean, the Turkish customs."

"Which did you call, Turkish customs or northern Cyprus?"

"I called Turkish customs and explained the situation to them."

"You didn't call the Turkish Republic of Northern Cyprus, did you?"

She answered that she understood that this entity was under the protection of Turkey.

"Who did you speak to when you called Turkish customs?" Kline asked.

"An official."

"You don't know the name?"

"I don't recall the name, no."

"Who did you speak with at Swiss customs?"

"I don't recall the name."

"Who did you speak to at customs in New York?"

"I don't recall the name."

They discussed her other inquiries for a while, and there was also something about her letters to Merchants National Bank failing to mention Michel van Rijn's financial interest in the transaction.

Then, out of the blue, Kline asked, "Miss Goldberg, would you identify Exhibit SS, please?"

"Yes. It is a fax from me to Mr. Frenzel and Mr. Massey at Merchants Bank marked URGENT with the descriptions or information that they had asked for."

"You wrote URGENT up at the top?"

"Yes."

"Would you turn to the very last paragraph on the second page just above THANKS AGAIN, and read that into the record, please."

"The last paragraph?"

"Yes. I'm sorry, I do have a clearer copy if it is helpful. I have the original fax." His hand seemed to tremble as he held it up.

"No, I can read it. That is all right." A hush fell over the courtroom. She read, " 'All are depicted in the publication of Dumbarton Oaks, a copy of which will be given to you upon my return.' "

"What do you recall to be the date of this letter?"

"I'm sorry, I can't read the date."

"There doesn't appear to be a handwritten date. Let me show you the original from the files of the Merchants National Corporation and ask you if this was not a letter that you transmitted to them by fax on July 5, 1988?"

"Yes."

"So, as of July 5, 1988, you were aware of the existence of the Megaw and Hawkins book published by Dumbarton Oaks concerning the Kanakariá mosaics?"

"No, I was not." Her answer seemed a bald denial of what she had just read aloud.

"You were aware that there was a publication from Dumbarton Oaks concerning the mosaics?" he repeated.

"I was aware that there was a publication that depicted the mosaics, yes," she said, apparently contradicting herself.

"And that it was from Dumbarton Oaks?"

"Yes."

"Do you recall that we discussed at your deposition the question of the existence of the Dumbarton Oaks publication?"

"Yes."

"Do you recall that you told me that you were not aware of the existence of the publication until you returned to the United States?"

"Yes."

"And learned about it some six weeks later?"

"Yes."

This exchange suggested a scenario—that in buying the mosaics Peg had been prompted by an illicit motive. The scenario, actually a combination of two classic confidence games, went like this: The Modigliani painting had been offered as the bait in a bait-and-switch scam, and when Peg rejected it, as she was meant to, she was unwittingly setting up Merchants for the kill. By not availing herself of the bank's first letter of reference, she had proved her self-restraint and thus ingratiated herself with Nick Frenzel, who was now predisposed to fork over hard cash for her next request. One had to picture her, jet-lagged and on heavy pain-killing drugs, limping about Amsterdam with one hand virtually in Merchants' vault; fancying herself shrewd in business, with no time to lose, and, like so many opportunistic people, blind to her own defects of judgment, she would have made a very ripe pigeon. The city's theatrical atmosphere provided all the necessary intoxication for the second act of the script—a classic bunco play in which the mark is shown some superb but relatively low-priced merchandise, clearly of suspicious origin, and is offered the opportunity to buy it. In this scheme, the goods soon turn out to be fake or too hot to resell, but in the meantime the bunco players shake off the mark, who is too cowed and embarrassed to seek help from the police. If Peg had known of the existence of the Dumbarton Oaks monograph, there was every reason to suppose that she had also suspected—perhaps without admitting it to herself—that the mosaics were stolen. Unlike most marks, however, she had waltzed right out into the limelight. Although, according to the con-game theory, the con stopped running when Peg discovered that she couldn't sell the stolen pieces, she was constrained to pretend it was running so as to make it seem that she hadn't played along with it; yet precisely this pretense of innocence would undermine her in court by making her seem a gullible buyer.

Kline carefully refrained from pressing home the thesis of her complicity in the fencing of the stolen mosaics—he couldn't prove it and didn't need it—but *The Indianapolis Star* felt no such compunction, and it stated flatly that Peg stood accused of "knowingly" buying plundered antiquities. She was also described in *The New York Times* as "pretending to believe a cock-and-bull story." By degrees, the trial was acquiring many of the attributes of a criminal proceeding.

Perhaps the most damaging document of the case against Peg was not the fax about the Dumbarton Oaks monograph, however. It was a purchase agreement, dated July 3, 1989, between Peg and the middlemen, which had been unearthed during the discovery process. This agreement showed that Peg paid $1.08 million for the mosaics, not the $1.2 million she received from Merchants National Bank; it thus appeared that she had used $120,000 for other purposes; however, she had shown her bank a fully executed bill of sale for $1.2 million, dated July 7. Thus it would be hard for the court not to conclude that she had knowingly participated in a contract bearing a false purchase price. She testified that she had told Nick Frenzel she would be withholding $120,000, but in his deposition he had claimed not to have known about this. Now, as her tale of how she had disposed of this sum grew fantastically complicated, Judge Noland totted up the figures on a pad. Kline's team noticed that he was no longer looking her in the eye.

There was another short period of questioning by Emerson, then an even shorter period of re-cross-examination by Kline. As Kline concluded, he asked her, "How many names has Robert Fitzgerald used during the time that you have known him?"

"Bob Jones or Robert Evan Jones, Robert E. Jones, Robert Fitzgerald, Fitzgerald Jones," she said.

"And Jones-hyphen-Fitzgerald?"

"Yes."

*   *   *

On August 3, 1989, Judge Noland handed down his decision and order: that the four mosaics belonged to the Church of Cyprus and should be delivered into the custody of that institution. Noland found that the law of Indiana should apply in the case: because the Church of Cyprus had never sold or given the mosaics to anyone, Peg had not acquired valid ownership of them. It was consequently unnecessary to determine whether she had bought the pieces in good faith, but Judge Noland went on to consider the issues "in the alternative"—that is, as if the law of Switzerland, the country where the transaction had taken place, were applicable. Here Peg's due diligence was a major factor, and he found it inadequate, stating six reasons for her to have been put off the purchase: that the mosaics came from a war-torn country in which the rule of law had for a while not prevailed; that the sacred and essentially architectural, or immovable, nature of the pieces offered grounds for caution and delay; that the disparity between the offering price and several appraisal valuations suggested a "hot" origin; that the seller's reputation was unknown to the buyer; that the middlemen were suspect; and, last, that she had concluded the purchase with undue haste. In essence, Peg Goldberg had not adequately considered whether Aydin Dikmen had title to the pieces, and her inquiry into their provenance had been slipshod.

There was nothing farfetched about Judge Noland's decision, but what he apparently did not suspect was that his judgment, if upheld, would end by creating a new set of international standards for the purchase of ancient art, since unknown provenance, artificially high appraisals, suspicious middlemen, and lightning transactions are the stuff of the antiquities trade.

3

Kline's cross-examination of Peg—what his colleagues at Manatt, Phelps had taken to calling the "cross of Goldberg"—was an unqualified disaster for her. Her testimony at that point helped cause her defeat, and she thereby lost the case, the mosaics, and a great deal of money. She later told me that she had replied in strict conformity with her lawyers' instructions, which, she insisted, she had found repugnant. One might wonder if this was correct—had her memory been distorted by defeat?—but she expressed herself with affecting ruefulness. She had been asked, she felt, to seem more guileless than she was, to wish away the dram of skepticism that had colored her first impressions of Michel van Rijn and Ronald Faulk, to suppress her valid, if often rather convoluted, explanations for going along with the peculiarities of the purchase. She told me that her lawyers had told her not to mention a certain lost briefcase containing the records of her pre-purchase inquiries into the legality of the acquisition, and not to expatiate on her "perfectly legitimate" business reasons for having over-borrowed by $120,000. She spoke of these matters in a distressed tone of voice, interspersing her phrases with sighs, yet she seemed to cling to her stubborn dream of righteous inviolability. It seemed that she felt she had somehow won, for surely the whole world could see that her opponents were "twits" and their arguments "retarded." She was little Peg, tilting against the provincial pieties of a city that failed to grasp the realities of commerce and the law.

Her arguments, if extravagant, were not altogether unconvincing. When I eventually obtained a copy of her famous fax to Merchants Bank about the Dumbarton Oaks monograph, its wording astonished me. There were a few introductory sentences, and then, under the heading "Description," it read: "3 of the 4 mosaics are approximately 40 x 50 cm. by 10–12 cm. thick, and according to experts who have carefully examined the pieces, represent (1) St. Mateos [St. Matthew] (2) St. Paul (3) St. Luke. 4th icon is larger, measuring 45 x 65 cm. x 12 cm. thick; it is extraordinarily rare, for it depicts Jesus as a young adolescent." A little farther down came the sentence that Tom Kline had asked Peg to read aloud in court: "All are depicted in the publication of Dumbarton Oaks, a copy of which will be given to you upon my return." The first amazing thing was the misidentification of two of the icons. The first of the four mosaics, of which Michel van Rijn had shown her photographs, clearly bore the inscription ΙΑΚΟΒΟC, and it would not have cost her many pains to look this up in a Greek dictionary and discover that it means "James." There was no excuse, either, for the mistaken notion that the figure with an angel's wing was a disciple, since his nimbus, unlike those of the disciples, carried no inscription. If Peg had examined the captions in the Dumbarton Oaks monograph she could have determined at once who the figures were.

But did she have the monograph at the time of the purchase? That's what I had begun to doubt. "A copy of which will be given to you upon my return" isn't a normal grammatical construction. Ordinarily, one would say, "a copy of which I shall give to you upon my return." Both her misidentification and her syntax suggested that she had not seen the book but merely knew vaguely of some sort of publication. And if this was true, then she had not lied to Kline when he quizzed her about it during her cross-examination: though she indeed knew of it, she had very little notion of what it was. Faulk, in his testimony, explicitly denied that she had seen the book, and when, as she stated in her deposition, she did procure a copy for herself, some six weeks after returning to the United States, she immediately told a dozen people about it in tones of the wildest delight. ("I know I sound brainless," Peg said to me once, "but when I bought those mosaics I didn't know what Dumbarton Oaks was.") Yet the misidentification of the pieces and the failure to specify the exact title and nature of the Dumbarton Oaks "publication" undermined her credibility as a responsible buyer. That, one might suppose, was why her own lawyer had not opted to dwell on this point: the less time devoted to that dreadful fax, the better.

It was through a long series of telephone conversations conducted while she was appealing Judge Noland's verdict that I really got to know Peg Goldberg. She was just a bright voice at the other end of the line, but a voice I listened to more and more often, and after a while I decided that I might just as well invest in a round-trip ticket to Indianapolis. When at last we met, I began by telling her some things about myself that I was sure she wasn't going to like. I told her that I had for many years been close to the family of a Greek priest in New York and was familiar, in a non-scholarly sort of way, with the Orthodox liturgy and the devotional use of icons; I told her that I knew something about the looting of northern Cyprus and regarded it as a cultural disaster of vast proportions. In short, I was not unhappy about Judge Noland's decision, and I thought that she had emerged from the trial in an oddly ambiguous light.

Prim with conviction, she heard me out coolly, then answered with a generosity that disarmed me. "I know that right now my reputation doesn't exactly look suitable for framing," she said. "But I really don't feel that I did any wrong. Do you think I would borrow over a million dollars in my own name and then go buy something I suspected was stolen? Is there anything in my record to suggest I'm retarded?" She explained how the trial had narrowed her future, maimed her faith in mankind. She felt handicapped and therefore defiant, and would welcome any effort at an objective clarification of the case. "I even have a letter from U.S. Customs affirming that the mosaics were legally imported," she said. "Don't I deserve the *Good Housekeeping* Seal of Approval for that one? If only the truth could finally come out, it would help make me whole again."

For a moment, embarrassed by my interloper status, I thought about the anguish she'd expressed. Then I said, "I don't know if any of us will ever get to the bottom of this puzzle. But if I do decide to write something about you, could you possibly come out of it looking any worse than you do now?"

She laughed one of her powerful laughs.

In the months that followed, I talked with many attorneys about the case, and I tried to pass on to Peg what I gathered from their explanations. There were good reasons why Joe Emerson might have wished that she seem competent and yet not too sophisticated. Then, too, a sea change was taking place in the world's conception of cultural patrimony; all the equities in the case—the informal policy concerns—argued for the restitution of the icons to the Church of Cyprus; American legal thought would always place a greater burden on the purchaser's moral responsibility to know what he was buying than on the victim's responsibility to broadcast word of his loss. For Peg, these matters were "mere emotionalism" or a "propaganda scenario" contrived by Greek Cyprus. When I dared to point out, as many of her friends already had, that to buy four icons stripped from an architectural site was an awfully risky business, she didn't seem fazed in the least. "What about all the Cypriot antiquities in the British Museum?" she would say, flapping a hand in the air. "What about the Cesnola Collection at the Met? Who arranged those—the antiquities fairies?"

Peg would talk for hours about the case, sitting with legs crossed on a sofa while shafts of sunlight stole imperceptibly around her huge living room and then died slowly away. Because the purchase was her idée fixe, she had become approachable from one angle only, like a statue in a niche. Surrounded by pieces of evidence—by tapes and clippings and faxes, and also by bank memos, because the case had left her in a financial bind—she would laughingly exclaim that she was "repaying the national debt." She now owed well over a million dollars to Nick Frenzel, who, conscious of his compromised position, had repaid her note to Merchants Bank and himself assumed the role of creditor. Often the phone rang, drowning out the robins on her lawn, and then she was obliged to announce herself with a name blackened in the world press. It might be Scotland Yard on the line, or the FBI, or any one of a host of people from Los Angeles to Istanbul who wanted to know more about the maze she bitterly continued to explore—the maze of the antiquities trade.

Largely because Peg suspected that Cypriot government officials had "dirty hands" in the whole affair and had in the past struck bargains with the Turkish gentleman, she appealed Judge Noland's verdict to the Seventh Circuit Court of Appeals. Above and beyond wanting to reverse the decision in favor of Cyprus, she was angry that the trial had never afforded a convincing model of what had actually happened to her, and that too many alarming omissions and mendacities had been passed over. When you studied all the testimony, the loose ends whipped you in the face. How much did Cyprus really know about the Turkish gentleman? Who had possession of the remaining mosaics? Who had severed the Hand and the Feet? Was Peg's story merely a subplot, a sealed-up room in some vast labyrinth of conspiracy, or was "conspiracy" not quite the right word? As she pressed forward with her inquiries, the affair took on broader dimensions than anyone had ever thought it would. Who stood behind the mosaics caper? Who had organized the looting of Byzantine Cyprus? Was there a vast secret alliance somewhere, or only criminal gangs, hidden factions, cells that endlessly bred and crossbred, perfidious and strife-torn?

The Turkish gentleman remained an enigma. In May 1989, in London, *The Independent* had published an article about the trial by its art-market correspondent, Geraldine Norman, who had evidently received some information from Michel van Rijn. Her report was illustrated with what purported to be an old photograph of Aydin Dikmen, and when Peg saw it, an eerie feeling came over her: she realized that this was not the man she had met at the Geneva airport—the elderly fellow with jaundice. Other people who had supposedly seen him gave varying accounts of his appearance. Bob Fitzgerald, who had encountered him fleetingly in Geneva, had said in his deposition that Dikmen was short and nearly bald. Faulk said that he was a healthy man in his fifties, with salt-and-pepper hair. The more you thought about Dikmen, the more you had to suspect that if such a person existed Peg had probably never clapped eyes on him. It seemed that somebody was trying to keep her away from the real Turkish gentleman, but if she was to be kept from him, why had she been told his name and address? It was silly; it didn't make sense.

Then, slowly, an insight matured in her, like a harvest long overdue. It was not so much that she had to be prevented from meeting Dikmen as that Dikmen had to be prevented from meeting her. Whoever he was, he probably wouldn't have sold the mosaics to her if he'd known the sort of person she was: an American, a woman, an innocent. An outsider.

*   *   *

One of the most bewildering aspects of the entire mosaics case was the refusal of people and events to fulfill the duties that one's imagination instinctively assigned them. Deviance lurked in classy social contexts, major players turned out to be stand-ins for others, a single deal might result in two conflicting contracts, and apparent conclusions, like the trial itself, developed into new beginnings. Temperamentally attracted to unpopular causes, Peg was now wedded to her own, and she might have been expected to nurse nothing but naked hatred for her two former friends Bob and Michel. Yet when I asked her how she felt about them, her reply threw me into perplexity. "Michel I suppose I could tear limb from limb, but Bob's another matter altogether. I just can't forget that Bob strongly encouraged me to check out the salability of the pieces. He thought I was a little nuts, of course, what with all those agencies I was phoning, but I clearly remember him sitting in the armchair in my hotel room in Geneva saying, 'Hey, take your time, make all the calls that you want.' "

More remarkable still was Peg's attitude toward the Turkish gentleman. His identity, of course, was exceedingly blurry: he wore several faces, misspelled his own name, and had sent her, through a veiled intermediary, title deeds to the mosaics signed by a supposed Turkish Cypriot official whose name oscillated between "General Osmeck" and "Osman Örek." Tom Kline, who after the trial had moved his practice to the Washington office of Andrews & Kurth, absolutely refused to concede that Dikmen was a flesh-and-blood person: Dikmen, he maintained, was no more than a useful construct, like a dummy company, and should be viewed as fictional until proven real.

(Once, when I was in Washington, I dropped by Kline's office to spout some goofy theory about the Turk, and Kline looked up at me with an impish smile and said, "Maybe *you're* Dikmen.") Peg naturally took the opposing view, that a real, live Dikmen had sold her the mosaics, and I always assumed unquestioningly that the Turk was a villain, a sort of ghoulie, in her private cosmology. I was taken aback when she said to me one evening over the phone, "I suppose this must seem funny to you, but I really like Aydin—I have no ill will toward him at all."

"But you've never met him!" I protested. "Not the real Aydin, anyway."

"Oh, I did, I did meet him," she replied. "I don't want to advertise this, but I went to see him a few months after the trial. At that time I was still smarting with outrage, I was looking for new evidence, so at first I tried to contact Michel. I telephoned a place called the ParkHotel, in The Hague, where I believed Michel was living, but he seemed to have recently decamped. Then Bob—Bob Fitzgerald—phoned me. He told me that somebody, some incoherent foreigner, had called him at his condo—I guess the foreigner had found Bob's number in Michel's abandoned address book in the hotel. And the funny thing was that the foreigner desperately wanted to talk to me. Knowing this gave me a creepy feeling, but pretty soon I got through to the man. He told me in broken English that he and some others knew of my predicament, that they sympathized deeply and wished to assist me, but for this I must first come to Holland. So in the fall of 1989 I took Jay Yeager, Emerson's associate, and went back to Amsterdam, back to the Marriott Hotel and its sidewalk café, where I met with three men who identified themselves as Michel's former body-guards."

Two of them, Peg told me, were Yugoslavs, whom I shall here call Marko and Draža; the third was a Dutchman, whom I'll call Hans. Offering to sell her documentary evidence supposedly damning for Cyprus's case, they asked for an astronomical sum of money, which she did not have. She returned home to Indiana, empty-handed and heavyhearted.

"A few weeks later," Peg continued, "Yeager and I went back to Amsterdam to parley again with Marko, Draža, and Hans. They'd promised to introduce me to someone of greater interest than themselves, and in hopes that this personage was Aydin Dikmen, I brought along an interpreter who knew both Turkish and German. If I recall correctly, the three of us went down at a prearranged hour to the Marriott lobby, where, to our amazement, we discovered a small crowd waiting for us. I was still half expecting to see the jaundiced sufferer I had met at the Geneva airport, so this crowd filled me with anxiety; I felt I was being drawn deeper and deeper into a nightmare. Besides the three bodyguards, there was, let me see, a fairish man with bangs, whom the others called Mehmet; an Asian with slicked-back hair and a long knife—no, a gun, in a shoulder holster; a short graying business type holding a briefcase; and a fellow I remember as very tall and dark, broad-shouldered and slim-waisted, who stood apart from the others, saying nothing.

"My glance was immediately attracted to the graying man with the briefcase. You see, his shoes were really good, and his suit was beautifully tailored. His haircut flattered his handsome face. Almost at once, I realized that I liked him—don't ask me why—and I also realized he was shouting at me. I asked my interpreter, 'What in heaven's name is he saying?' and the interpreter said, 'He's asking in Turkish if you've ever met him before.' I said, 'Tell him I don't know! Tell him I can't remember!'

"But the elegant man railed on, making lots of fierce gestures. 'If the lady never met me before,' he said, through my interpreter, 'then why did she use my name? Why ruin my business? Why get me in trouble with the tax authorities?' He looked furious, but behind the outrage in his eyes I thought I detected something else—anxiety, vulnerability, bewilderment, as if he were adrift in a world he couldn't fathom and was beseeching me, of all people, to help him. I held out my hand, but he refused it.

"What happened next? Well, I recall that I took a small English-German dictionary out of my purse and, summoning a remnant of my college German, slowly composed a sentence. I said, 'I have never seen you before'—though in a way, I realized, I had, in that photograph in *The Independent*. Digging into my purse again, I held up a copy of the $1.2 million bill of sale for the mosaics and pointed to his signature. 'Mr. Dikmen,' I said, 'you signed this paper.' I waited for him to grasp what I meant, then moved my finger briskly upward to the document's warranty—the warranty against impediments to sale."

As Peg remembered it, the man whom she so casually identified as Dikmen appeared to understand the gravity of the situation, and the group retired to a conference room—a one-bedroom suite she'd booked for the occasion. The discussion resumed, and in the course of it "Dikmen" told a story of ancient rivalries and government corruption, and of how in the midst of it all he had obtained official permission to salvage endangered church art in northern Cyprus; he was, he said, just an innocent restorer of antiquities. Sometimes during the meeting, Peg became aware that the tall dark man who had stood apart in the lobby seemed to exercise a certain authority: though he said nothing, he was closely observing the proceedings. After a while, as if by a prearranged signal, the group walked out of the suite, and finally, Peg's interpreter requested a break.

Peg and "Dikmen" were now alone, with no common language—his German wasn't much better than hers—yet with a shared sensation of having a world of things to say to each other. It was like a fairy tale in which people transformed into beasts desperately try to communicate. Peg watched as the Turk, now in pantomime, now in disjointed German, tried to convey his thoughts: he seemed to be asserting that he had never been involved in the mosaics transaction, that he had never sold her a thing. A word formed on her lips, the kind of word she didn't use often. "Bullshit!"

At this, Peg told me, his eyes widened and grew troubled. So he knew some English after all! Would he understand more? She went over to the bed and unfolded on it a newspaper she had brought with her. It contained an article about the case, and Peg summarized in simple sentences what the columns said: that she, who was not a rich woman, had bought something that she would probably not be allowed to keep; that she had lost more than a million dollars. She also tried to make him understand that she was a decent person and that she was very sorry if she had caused him any pain.

"Then he sat down beside me on the bed," Peg told me. "With a deep sigh he looked up at me and made what I suppose was a supreme effort to speak in my language. 'Lady Goldberg,' he began, and then stopped.

" 'Yes?' I said.

" 'Lady Goldberg, Popps is a liar!' And all at once he was on his feet again, his face contorted with rage, spewing out all his bitterness at the humiliation he'd suffered at the hands of the man he called 'Popps.' When I pointed out that Walter Hopps, under oath, had basically just repeated Yanni Petsopoulos's silly story about getting hold of some of the Kanakariá mosaics for Cyprus, Dikmen's eyes blazed at the sound of the Greek name, and he looked like he'd spit on the carpet. 'Popps was my guest!' he shouted. '*My guest!*' Then he stopped for a moment to catch his breath. 'Does anyone really believe,' he asked me, 'that Vassos Karageorghis and Constantine Leventis do not know me? That Karageorghis has never done business with me?' He was still shaking his head. 'Cyprus,' he said, almost groaning. 'It is such a small island. How could an American judge believe these things?'

"I said to him, 'Aydin, why didn't you come to Indianapolis and defend yourself? Why didn't you come and help *me?*' "

But here, according to Peg, their exchange broke down, for he replied in a babel of languages. He told her that her defeat was foreordained, it was kismet— the Greek Cypriots had worked the whole thing out in advance. And Michel van Rijn had told him that if he, Aydin, went to America, he would be arrested and thrown into prison.

Presently the others returned, and the interpreter helped to calm the Turk down, calling him "Aydin Bey," as one would a person of consequence. Mollified, "Dikmen" promised to put Peg in touch with a certain Turkish Cypriot who had all the information she needed. In return, she gave him a signed statement to the effect that he was not the man she had met in Geneva the previous year; as a precautionary measure she also gave a $5,000 tip to the three intimidating bodyguards. All of them made ready to leave, but before the meeting broke up, something curious happened. The dark, broad-shouldered fellow who had been sitting off to one side got up and introduced himself to her as "Benjamin." He was, he said, a Yugoslav; he had come to the conclusion that she was an honorable person, and he promised to do his very best to help her. "This really puzzled me," Peg said, "and later, when the whole group had left, I asked the interpreter if he'd discovered anything about this mysterious man. 'I would do my very utmost to avoid him,' said the interpreter. 'Aydin is afraid of him. Aydin says that this Yugoslav has him under surveillance, under virtual house arrest. Aydin says that he is Mafia.' "

Like Aydin Dikmen, Benjamin lived in Munich, and in March 1990 he arranged in that city a second meeting between Peg and the man she believed to be Dikmen. Peg related to me that she flew in and stayed at the Bayerischer Hof—alone this time, and more afraid than ever. "Dikmen" graciously called at the hotel and drove her through town to a Balkan restaurant, grinding the gears of his Mitsubishi sedan, cutting corners, racing the wrong way up a one-way street. He seemed "afraid of his own shadow," as Peg put it to me, and she sensed that he suspected they were being followed. Benjamin met them at the restaurant, and during their three-way conversation, as she recalled it, the Turk admitted for the first time that he had sold her the mosaics. He told her that he had not known at the time of the sale that she was the buyer, and that if he had known he would not have sold them to her for all the tea in China. In fact, he had believed he was selling them to Cyprus, in the person of Constantine Leventis, who, he said, had paid him about 180,000 Deutsche marks in 1984 for four other Kanakariá mosaics (this was obviously a reference to the roundels depicting Saint Jude and Saint Bartholomew, and the two fakes). He also told her that he had netted $150,000 out of the sale, not the $350,000 that had been mentioned at the trial.

As she listened, Peg experienced a brief moment of elation. After all, Leventis had testified at the trial that he had no knowledge of Aydin Dikmen until a few months earlier, and that Saints Jude and Bartholomew had been *given* back, not purchased. But to her disappointment, "Dikmen" also told her that he had torn up the signed statement she had given him in Amsterdam a few weeks before. For reasons he left unstated, it had not satisfied him, and it certainly hadn't induced him to befriend her. Peg still liked the beautifully groomed Turk—he was such a gentleman!—but now she thought she discerned in him an obsessive fondness for secrecy.

He offered her no immediate aid, regretting that he did not have any documents that would be of use to her, but as he had promised, he did give her the phone number of a very knowledgeable Turkish Cypriot, a trader named Ahmet, who apparently possessed various orders and invoices for antiquities bearing the signature of Vassos Karageorghis. Ahmet knew everything, the Turk said; Ahmet was the key person for her. Ignoring her pleas for help, "Dikmen" wanted to talk only about what he had rescued from vandals in northern Cyprus; about how everybody in the antiquities world had known of his Cypriot inventory; and about all the treasures he had sold to American museums and colleges. Peg said goodbye to him with the feeling that he was wounded and intractable.

One thing, however, cheered her: during her stay in Munich, Benjamin had afforded her a certain hospitality and protection. She felt her fear of him slowly ebbing, and then, to her amazement, he suddenly offered to help her overturn the decision of the Indianapolis court. By no means coarse or menacing, and surprisingly knowledgeable about art history, he told her that his real name was Savo Kujundzic, and that he was simply a hydraulics engineer who happened to be fond of paintings and objets d'art.

Within weeks of her return to Indianapolis, Benjamin, or, more properly, Savo, turned up at her doorstep, offering to be deposed by her lawyers. His participation in the appeals process took a long time to arrange, however, in part because Joe Emerson was more than a little skeptical of all these omniscient foreigners. "Bad people, Peg," he would say, shaking his head. He insisted to her that Savo resembled a Hollywood thug, what with his dark suit and white socks, whereupon Peg pointed out that Savo's suit was of the best Italian silk and had probably cost over fifteen hundred dollars, and that white socks worn with black trousers were all the rage among the smarter Continental men that year. So by the time Savo's statement came to be taken, in May 1990, Tom Kline declared that it was absurdly late—"untimely," as lawyers say—and that the plaintiffs would boycott it. It turned into a videotaped proceeding, at which none of Cyprus's lawyers was present.

Under oath, Savo contemptuously dismissed the rumor that he was some sort of crook. He said that he had gone to school in Hjevlja, in Montenegro, where he had excelled in mathematics; had received a diploma in mechanical engineering from the University of Belgrade, in 1979; had done postgraduate work at the Sorbonne for two years; had for several years represented a German hydraulics company in Yugoslavia; and had then moved to Munich and founded a small firm specializing in the design of hydraulic and pneumatic guidance systems. In 1978, he said, he met Aydin Dikmen, in Belgrade, where Dikmen was buying ships for scrap metal (this business about scrap metal chimed with what Michel van Rijn had told Peg about Dikmen, way back in Amsterdam, at the very beginning of the case), and had seen Dikmen regularly since moving to Munich. Dikmen had introduced himself to Savo as a former archaeologist with a particular interest in the prehistory of the Danube basin, and also as a collector of idols, coins, ceramics, sculptures, and all sorts of Greek, Roman, and Byzantine items. According to Savo, Dikmen had owned property in both the north and south of Cyprus before the 1974 Turkish invasion, and had been well known to Vassos Karageorghis. After the invasion, Savo said, Dikmen had obtained permission from the Turkish authorities to "save" various frescoes and mosaics in the north from dereliction and perhaps from complete destruction.

Savo also seemed to know a great deal about the Kanakariá mosaics that were still missing—Saints Andrew, Thomas, and the Hand and Feet. When Emerson asked him if he knew their whereabouts, he replied, cryptically, "Mr. Dikmen no longer has them. They don't belong to him. Mr. Dikmen has no mosaics at all anymore," and when Emerson again asked him, "Do you know where they are?" Savo said, "Yes, but I would prefer not to answer that."

At the trial, the Republic of Cyprus had claimed that it had failed to go after the mosaics because it didn't know who had them, but Savo said that Cyprus had known exactly who had them. He stated that he had met with Dikmen, the London dealer Yanni Petsopoulos, a restorer named Stavros Mihalarias, and Constantine Leventis sometime in the early 1980s, at Sotheby's, in London, where Leventis had attempted to negotiate a purchase of the Byzantine frescoes from the little church near Lysi. Dikmen and Leventis had seemed at variance, Savo recalled, with Petsopoulos desperately trying to mediate between them. A couple of months later, he said, Dikmen and Leventis again met in his presence, and it was obvious to him from their discussion that Leventis had already bought some of the Kanakariá mosaics from Dikmen. Savo's description of these personalities was uncannily accurate (except for his version of Leventis, which seemed a little off the mark), and on August 3, 1990, one year to the day after Judge Noland had ruled in favor of Cyprus, Joe Emerson filed a motion to set aside judgment, based on Savo's sworn statement. Tom Kline was more than a little worried, but three months later, the motion was denied. Judge Noland found that Savo's statement, even if wholly true, did not radically undermine the Cypriot case. (The Court of Appeals, meanwhile, had upheld Noland's original decision.)

Still convinced that she was in the right, however, Peg found vastly more powerful representation in the Washington firm of Arnold & Porter, which is on retainer to the American Association of Dealers in Ancient, Oriental, and Primitive Art. Her new strategy was to contest the Church of Cyprus's ownership of the pieces before the Supreme Court of the United States, on the ground that they had been expropriated by Turkish Cyprus after the 1974 invasion; naturally Arnold & Porter was delighted to contemplate the possibility of engaging in a round of historic litigation. The firm plainly believed that her case was a strong one; but how was she meeting her legal expenses? On the Greek Cypriot side, the fear grew that she was secretly being funded by Turkey.

When, fascinated by the thought that Peg would actually bring her case before the highest court in the land, I telephoned her to ask who was paying Arnold & Porter, she replied that she was not yet at liberty to tell me, but that all might be revealed in the fullness of time. It was with coy pleasure, I felt, that she wrapped herself in the mantle of mystery, but in truth there was mystery and dubiety on all sides. Shortly before the Indianapolis trial, for example, Emerson had informed the Cypriots that he wished to take the deposition of Vassos Karageorghis—who, as a noted archaeologist and the Cypriot Director of Antiquities from 1963 to 1989, might be expected to have known of Aydin Dikmen; inexplicably Karageorghis had never shown up, and Leventis had appeared in his place. Now, however, reports in two serious journals, one Turkish and one American, contradicted Leventis's claim that no money had been paid for the mosaics that were returned to Cyprus in 1984. Peg herself also came into possession of a tape in which Michael Kyprianou, a member of the Cypriot parliament and an attorney on retainer to the Church of Cyprus, could be heard chatting and laughing with Michel van Rijn, asking for his aid in the recovery of stolen Cypriot art. If Cyprus was negotiating with Michel, she reasoned, it could very well have negotiated with Aydin Dikmen. It seemed that Dikmen's activities were not unknown in his part of the world. Özgen Acar, a Turkish journalist who had made a study of Balkan smuggling routes, had in mid-1989 written a series of articles on the looting of Cyprus for the Istanbul daily *Cumhuriyet,* in which he pointed out that Dikmen had made headlines in the Turkish press in March 1977 in connection with twenty-one illegally exported Cypriot icons. The daily *Hürriyet* had even printed a photograph of Dikmen's private museum, in Konya. It was absurd to suppose that the Greek Cypriots did not monitor such reports.

The role of the dealer Yanni Petsopoulos also excited Peg's curiosity. It was interesting, of course, that Petsopoulos seemed to know so much about Dikmen's stock, but what was even more interesting was the insouciance with which he had apparently gone about

rescuing the Lysi frescoes. According to the trial testimony of Cyprus's star expert witness Gary Vikan,
Petsopoulos, before approaching the Menil Foundation with his putative discovery, had appeared at
Dumbarton Oaks and offered the frescoes to Vikan,
who was then a senior associate there. He had shown
Vikan some questionable documentation and a crude
rendering (apparently by Dikmen) of a fictional
church whose walls the frescoes had supposedly
graced, and told him—with no attempt to distance
himself from the account—Dikmen's cover story that
he had found them in Turkey during the construction
of a hotel. The price was $600,000. Vikan informed
the court that he had taken the pieces to be "illicit
antiquities" and had flatly told Petsopoulos as much.
Yet the dealer had reappeared some weeks later at the
Menil Foundation and made a similar pitch to Walter
Hopps, who initially wanted nothing to do with him.

The stain of doubt was now threatening to be-
smirch everyone involved in the affair, and a whole
crowd of journalists and legal experts and amateur
conspiracy theorists began to float hypotheses concerning what had actually been going on. They called
themselves "Kanakariá junkies," and when they got
together their blood raced and their features took on
a ferretlike sharpness and they talked out of the sides
of their faces. One of them was myself, of course; by
now I phoned Peg at least once a week.

The junkies had noticed some interesting peculiarities. One was Mrs. de Menil's disclosure in her deposition that on her foray to Dikmen's Munich flat, in
1983, she had acquired two objects besides the Lysi
frescoes, one of them a jewel-studded Sumerian idol.
Yet if she harbored serious suspicions as to Dikmen's

honesty, as she also stated in her deposition, why had she bought these other items from him? How could she be sure that they, too, were not smuggled or stolen? And why, believing herself to know both the whereabouts and the possessor of valuable stolen property, had she neglected to notify the Munich police? Was she unaware of the ethical implications of such behavior? Actually, nothing in Mrs. de Menil's conduct could have come as a surprise to those who knew about her patronization of the late George Zacos, one of the most charming and learned of the old generation of Greek merchant-smugglers trained in the Grand Bazaar. One day in the summer of 1979, for example, she acquired from Zacos antiquities worth $120,000 for her future museum, and bought several Byzantine bowls as well, at $18,000 a throw, for some of her relatives; as usual, she requested no provenance documentation, and seemed unaware that Turkey had forbidden the exportation of all antiquities since Ottoman times.

The Kanakariá junkies also noticed that the Getty Museum, which in 1989 had alerted Cyprus to Peg Goldberg's possession of the mosaics, was itself the owner of a valuable Chalcolithic idol illicitly excavated in northern Cyprus, as well as two important antiquities, a statue of Aphrodite and a krater decorated by the great Greek painter Euphronios, believed by Italian authorities to have been illegally exported from their country. The junkies toyed with scores of logically possible but unproved scenarios. They wondered, for instance, whether agents of the Republic of Cyprus had organized the whole Kanakariá business from the start, commissioning the theft of the mosaics, then running four of them through the United

States as a propaganda coup against Turkey. Or whether the Greek Cypriots had lost their leverage over the thieves at some point, so that the mosaics fell into the wrong hands and the Republic of Cyprus was obliged to sue for their recovery.

There remained, of course, the con-game theory, which had much to recommend it. It was fairly tidy, it satisfied the lawman's and the newsman's cynical view of human nature, and it conveniently declared the loser guilty. In my own inquiry, I found it to be the prevalent view of the case, and I went along with it myself until a few details started to bother me. According to this theory, Peg Goldberg had knowingly bought hot goods, which she later discovered were too hot to unload openly, but she had also shelled out too much money to ditch them on the black market without sustaining a crippling loss. In effect, she was the "tail-end Charlie." What one might have expected, then, was that she would patiently try to sell them for a passable price to some very discreet or distant buyer—say, some Japanese. Yet she had unabashedly approached both the Getty and the Metropolitan Museum. If she had ever known or suspected that the pieces were stolen, she seemed to have somehow forgotten it.

And then there was Bob Fitzgerald's weird role. In September 1989, he had been charged with conspiracy in the 1984 burglary of an Indiana art collector's home, but the trial had been repeatedly postponed, and the prosecution's case against him depended largely on the testimony of two convicted felons who had turned state's witnesses. Bob himself had no rap sheet; and rumors were circulating at the time of the trial that he and his Idaho friend Lynn Harris had both worked for the CIA, either as informants or as operatives. ("Hell, no," Bob said when I asked him if this was true.) To me, Bob seemed a gambler, a poker player, a high-stakes, maximum-dare kind of dude, and not a professional criminal. He'd described himself to me as a hustler, and he certainly had the hustler's code of conduct: when he had told the court that his commission on the mosaics deal was none of Peg's business, he meant it quite literally. The deal was like a card game: the deck wasn't loaded; why should she get a peek at his hand? "Peg's a big girl, and very cunning," he told me once. "I suppose she hates me now, but I respect her anyway, and do you know why? Because she loves her cats."

As for Michel van Rijn—whose whereabouts were now uncertain—I'd never met him, but I couldn't see why he was so proprietary about the mosaics, and so interested in reuniting the far-flung pieces, if he thought that they couldn't be sold. What seemed more likely was that Fitzgerald and van Rijn and maybe some other unseen players simply hadn't attended to the issue of whether the mosaics could be resold legally or not; it may have been too fine a point for them—one that only a ruling from on high could decide. So they had done what speculators usually do on the threshold of a dangerous venture: they had induced somebody else to borrow the money, got somebody else to carry the note. Later, upset by the way things were going, they had bailed out.

In the spring of 1991, the Supreme Court declined to hear Peg's appeal. Her beloved archangel and the other three mosaics were languishing in a vault in Indianapolis until the Cypriots should determine how best to bring them home. Yet she still talked a lot about "my mosaics" and told me that she often dreamed about the archangel, and before I knew it, I too, was dreaming about the mosaics affair—around once a week, to be exact. I dreamed that aliens, androids, were behind the whole thing, directing its progress with the aid of a huge triangle of white fire; I dreamed that a priest in a long vestment and a conical miter was sitting atop a ladder under a dome, crooking his finger at me and urging me, enjoining me to—what? What was he babbling about?

I figured that Michel van Rijn knew as much as anyone about the story of the mosaics, and one evening at Bob Fitzgerald's favorite tavern in Indianapolis I started plying Bob with questions about him. But Bob, who had recently been divorced from his young wife, Barbara, and was spending less time than he wanted to with little Evan, hardly heard me. He was looking fondly at every kid who came into the place, thinking—it was obvious—about Evan. "Don't talk to me about Michel," he said.

"Why not?" I asked. "Is something the matter?"

"Michel's a karate champion, did you know that?"

"I've heard that, yes."

"Well, I don't consider myself any weakling, either. Last time he was here in Indianapolis, we got into an argument, and he took a poke at me. I got a shiner and he got a shiner." Bob rolled his eyes in disgust. "I think he had a difficult childhood, and he himself is a good father, which I respect. But one thing about Michel—he thinks kindness is weakness. And that really bothers me, it does."

I considered all this for a moment. Then I asked, "Do you know where Michel is right now?"

"I wish I didn't," Bob said. "But I do."

4

The Hotel des Indes, in The Hague, is a splendid glass-domed palace, a relic of the last century. Approaching it in a taxicab one afternoon in the spring of 1991, I saw two highly theatrical figures on the steps leading up to its ornate portal. One wore the uniform of a field marshal, circa 1890—he, I figured, was the doorman—and the other wore the costume of an art dealer from some voguish New York hangout of the late 1960s, like Max's Kansas City. It was hard to tell who wore more gold: the doorman had his gold buttons and braid and epaulets, but the art-dealer person had his own gold buttons, and a gold tie clasp and some other gold jewelry, all very brilliant. He had a Liberty hankie flying from his breast pocket. He wore a generously cut double-breasted jacket striped in several colors, a bright-yellow figured tie, a blue-and-white-striped shirt with flashing white collar and cuffs, pink suspenders, a great schoolboy shock of brown hair, and the sort of thick, flamboyant mustache that is de rigueur in certain lagoons of the art trade. The doorman leaped forward to open the cab door while I shuffled a blur of unfamiliar Dutch banknotes and tried to avoid looking at Michel van Rijn.

Later, when we got to know each other, Michel reproached me for this brief moment of avoidance in greeting him, but the truth was that he had given me a jolt. In photographs I had seen, he appeared as a handsome, powerfully built man in beautiful soft English clothes, the eyes hypnotic, Svengali-like, and whereas I could see that he had once looked like this, he had changed a great deal. He had become stout, and his face looked puffy. His bangs had grown long and swept down over one eye like a protective screen, leaving the other, naked eye to fend for itself. This eye now trained itself upon me, expectant, welcoming, but also measuring and doubting.

Michel loved attention, he loved journalists, and they were often in attendance. No one could accuse him of not being good copy: your rendezvous with Michel might begin with a trip to some exotic city, a wait in the gilded lobby of some grand hotel, a fast drive in a long black car to a secret luxury flat, where his stunning girlfriend—his girlfriend for *that* city, *that* week—would be throwing a soirée for a heterogeneous crowd of circus folk, bookmakers, industrialists, fashionable chefs, girls in silk tops wearing Opium, smooth-mannered young men of uncertain métier. And after a time Michel would make his appearance, irresistibly charming and generous. With some reason, he fancied himself a born storyteller, and as other rich men keep a houseboy or a valet, he kept a Cambridge-educated writer, a sort of Boswell, on lease; this writer would follow him about, all over the world, recording his escapades and bons mots. The upshot was a big volume of ghostwritten memoirs which, though still unpublished, had already been read by many people, and of which I possessed a racy digest.

Since I urgently needed to talk to him, I had obtained his telephone number and called him up. Then, without ever having seen me, he had got into the habit of placing transatlantic calls to me at least once a week, to offer breathless, rapid-fire information about smuggling from Argentina, or the wickedness of the great auction houses, or the Cypriots' efforts to recover their purloined art. After a while, I called up Scotland Yard to find out if this single human being could really have his finger in such an infinity of pies. "He's one of the top men in his line," a detective said, in a tone of grudging admiration. "He's had a hand in a lot of the world's art-smuggling jobs, and he'd be very happy to claim he had a hand in all of them." By degrees I gathered a considerable quantity of information about Michel, which I typed up and placed in a thick black dossier.

On our first afternoon together, we walked about The Hague, as we would do each day for the better part of a week. Carrying a portable phone to keep in touch with the worldwide art bazaar, Michel lumbered resolutely and unceasingly forward, along winding canals and over arched footbridges. He spoke of sparkling deals in such intimate detail that I was almost embarrassed; since I hardly knew him, this uncalled-for familiarity made me feel as if his voice had turned on automatically, triggered by a sensory mechanism that could detect a human presence. He bought and sold toys now; he bought and sold paint-

ings, music boxes, mechanical organs, steam callio-
pes, architectural fragments, Old Master drawings—
what didn't he buy and sell?

After taking me on an hour's forced march, Michel
started talking about the Kanakariá case. The sale to
Peg Goldberg had been a piece of cake, he recalled.
"She had that letter offering three million pounds,
and I certainly wasn't going to let her get away without selling her *something!*" He flashed an incisory
smile.

"How much did she know about the pieces?" I
asked.

"She knew exactly what they were," he said.

It was a cleverly ambiguous reply. When I pressed
him to explain himself, he said, "I gave her a copy of
the Dumbarton Oaks book." Since Peg had denied
having seen this monograph until well after her purchase of the mosaics, the two were nose to nose on
this point, as on so much else.

In the beginning, Michel said, Peg had fully grasped
the riskiness of the venture, but then, progressively
forgetting that the holy merchandise had to be disposed of quietly and discreetly, she had started listening to the art-market experts and had ended up asking
$20 million for the four pieces, including the archan-
gel she so desperately loved. Her ambition had made
her forget, Michel said: she refused to know what she
knew. "The trouble with Peg is that she wants to be
taken as this woman with a heart of gold, living in a
house full of rescued cats. But that is not at all who
she is. It's a mask."

Michel had barely launched into his account of the
mosaics and their peregrinations before he dropped it
and went on to something else. He began singing the

praises of the two most celebrated icon panels that had passed through his hands: a Saint Peter now in the British Museum and another Saint Peter at Dumbarton Oaks. It seemed that Aydin Dikmen had sold him the former, saying that it had come from a monastery in northern Cyprus, and van Rijn had passed it on to the London restorer Stavros Mihalarias, who had cleaned it and sold it to the museum for a glorious £175,000.

The Dumbarton Oaks Saint Peter, which Michel called "the crown of my Cyprus collection," had been a more complicated business. "I used to get things from a Greek thief, a very poor and very brave man, who would spend months making plans to steal icons from Greek monasteries," he told me. "He showed that one to me in Munich, and even the old wood was lovely, exquisite to the touch. I asked him if I could sleep with it in my room for a night—one must sleep with the things that one loves, no?—and so I was able to open my eyes and see it first thing next morning." Later he had lost the panel in a debt settlement, and it had gone to a Dutch businessman, who advertised it in the United States; eventually Gary Vikan—unaware that it was stolen—arranged to buy it for Dumbarton Oaks, where he then worked as an associate curator.

That afternoon it was drizzling. We looked at the rain-blurred ducks in the canals, we went in and out of damp little shops, and everywhere everyone hailed Michel. He was on the warmest terms with the whole town. Soon it grew dark, and he suggested that we "go through the courtesies," as he put it, and get drunk together.

No matter how much I drink, I cannot get properly,

merrily drunk—my mind goes blank, and I stare numbly ahead—but I saw no harm in joining him for a few rounds of geneva and fresh green herring. It began to pour, and we sat down in a pub overlooking a canal and contemplated the sheets of rain marching over the footbridge beside us.

We chatted about this and that—Michel was amusing, comradely—and then, after two or three glasses, he said quietly, "That Saint Peter in Dumbarton Oaks must go back to Greece. I will work for this—it must go home. Such a beautiful, beautiful painting. I know that Melina"—I assumed he meant Melina Mercouri, who was then Greece's Minister of Culture—"will insist on it."

This seemed the declaration of a chameleon-self, and perplexed by his motives, I studied his one naked eye: it bored back into me with what felt, all at once, like a manic intensity, fiery, searching, searching—but for what? Some piratical intent, some barely hatched journalistic perfidy? His eye was the color of the shadows in the tavern, bistre, dark and rich, and I grew aware that we'd had quite a lot to drink already; I remembered that this was something Bob Fitzgerald found disagreeable in Michel, Bob who drank sparingly and then only of the finest vintages.

I have only the dimmest memory of the evening that followed: quantities of intoxicants, pubs, tables, streets, footbridges, gables jumping in and out of the shadows; we had dinner and wine, and a pretty girl was conjured out of nowhere to show me a black dossier, rather thick, bearing my own name. Everyone we met—and we met many people—was a great friend of Michel's, and several times, on the crest of various bridges, I heard references to the mosaics and the names Peg Goldberg and Judge Noland, accompanied by screams of laughter. Wherever we went, we were followed by a gigantic chauffeur in a slowly moving car, and it was thanks to this personage that I returned, much ravaged, to my hotel in Amsterdam.

Before arriving in Holland I had secured from Peg, who had presumably got it from Savo, the telephone number of Marko, Draža, and Hans. Like any reporter, I wanted to hear all sides of the story, and the following evening I called the number from my hotel. A recorded announcement came on, informing me that I had reached a car phone and that the line was occupied. I repeated this several times, then telephoned a few times over the next few days, but always I received the same message. Usually I called in the evening, in the lonely circle of light cast by my bedside lamp, and each time I felt tenser, more jittery: I took it for granted that bodyguards carried weapons, and Peg had described Draža as a "very big boy." Nonetheless, I continued to dial the number at regular intervals—driven, I suppose, by the same relentless curiosity that had dragged me into this business in the first place.

Michel, meanwhile, entrusted me with a complete copy of his autobiography, and over the next few days I read it. It recounted, at a headlong pace, his initiation as a teenager into the Levantine icon trade, his early purchases in Soviet Armenia, his prankish bulk sales of "Mothers of God" to uninformed Japanese, his expansion into the illicit Cypriot antiquities traffic. The autobiography also told of Michel's first meeting, in the 1970s, with Aydin Dikmen, who had recently moved to Munich; of Dikmen's lofty claim to be rescuing Cypriot church treasures from looters and vandals; and of some dark dispute between him and Michel over an option to dispose of the Lysi frescoes. Was all of it true, or some of it, or none of it? Checking some episodes against information I already possessed, I found them partly confirmable. But key assertions hung on hearsay or rumor or the recollection of long-past events or, as it seemed to me, a farceur's feeling for story line.

Despite his talent for commerce and considerable personal wealth, Michel did not seem chiefly driven by the desire for boodle. Some other motive propelled him, perhaps a delight in game playing and hoodwinking, which for his breed of dealer was part of the order, even the decorum, of business. He was so fond of quick changes, switcheroos, pennyweightings, and counterfeits that none of the many hats he wore seemed decisively real to himself. When we met again in The Hague, I found myself smiling shamefacedly at his false-bottomed anecdotes, yet always under his laughter I heard a note of entreaty: to see him not as a mere fixer, a blowhard, but as a champion of the common man against the tartufferie of the museum people and big auctioneers. His book, he told me, would discredit these phony experts. "I make a fight with the hypocrites, I make a fight with Sotheby's," he said, clenching his fist in the gladiatorial salute.

I did not wish to become part of Michel's story, I wished to maintain a passable objectivity; but Michel would have none of it. There was no form of relation to him, least of all that of the itinerant chronicler, which he could not instantly personalize—this belonged to his method. Whatever he said to you somehow included and celebrated you, you were a part of its syntax, and in return you could not escape some feeling that you were applauding or at least winking at his unorthodox business methods. After all, he was personable and urbane, and just to smile at his jokes was to become, ever so slightly, a part of his operation.

"Michel," I said to him one day, "in your book you've revealed an awful lot about your illicit deals. I suppose that by your standards this information is already a little old, but still, what effect will all this have on your reputation?"

He smiled boyishly. "The effect will be devastating," he said.

"What will you do?"

"I'll choose a new identity, a new address. I'll use other faces. One is always a little bit the *comédien*, yes?"

That day we went for a stroll in The Hague, and at length we came to the park behind Queen Beatrix's palace. Michel pointed out some squarish objects suspended high in the trees above us: they were electronic sensors positioned there to detect prowlers in the neighborhood. Two years earlier, the palace's security measures had proved a blessing to him, he said, because he had taken a suite in the ParkHotel, right over there beyond the trees, so that he need not be afraid of snipers.

Why snipers? Well, that was a long and complicated business. According to Michel, an underworld figure named Max had made threats against him, and consequently he had enlisted the aid of three bodyguards who ran a protection racket—a pair of Yugoslavs called Marko and Draža, and a Dutchman called Hans. At the sound of these names I stopped dead in my tracks, but thought better of revealing my surprise and walked on. The three brought problems of their own, Michel said. They weren't satisfied with his payments—they were trying to extort more money than he had—and so, in desperation, he sold them shares in the resale value of one of the Kanakariá mosaics, the so-called Hand of Mary and Feet of Christ, which he had obtained from Aydin Dikmen. Then they moved into his suite, to make sure that he didn't abscond with the treasure. So there he was, a prisoner in his own abode, hanging on to the Feet of Christ for dear life. And in the midst of all this, Dikmen, who had become furious at him for raking so much off the proceeds of the sale to Peg Goldberg (and also for revealing Dikmen's name to Geraldine Norman, the art-market correspondent for *The Independent*), put a hired assassin on his case. The killer was called something like "Dujan"—all the Yugoslav hoodlums in Holland went by single code names. So, by degrees, life lost its sweetness, what with Max, Marko, Draža, Hans, and Dujan all persecuting Michel, and in August 1989 he just skipped out and caught a plane to Curaçao.

Before leaving, however, he tried to effect a reconciliation with Dikmen, explaining to him that if Peg won the trial in Indianapolis, the Kanakariá pieces still in the Turk's possession could be sold on the open market for millions of dollars. Dikmen replied that his own name must be cleared—if not, he'd put an end to Michel—but he did relent just enough to dispatch an associate to Holland to look into the possibility of a commercial alliance. He had understood that he, Michel, and Peg might soon be able to pool their holdings and market an incomparable set of masterworks.

"Dikmen's associate was another Yugoslav," Michel said, with a grimace. "He went by the code name of Benjamin."

"What was his real name?" I asked.

"It was Savo. I didn't like him. He was based in Munich and had some sort of tie-in to the mob. His connection with Dikmen I never understood."

I asked Michel to tell me more about Savo, and he rewarded me with a flashy anecdote. It seemed that one day Savo had notified him that he was taking a certain train from Munich to Amsterdam with the aim of smuggling an Impressionist painting into Holland. Michel found his candor appallingly stupid—"I mean," he explained to me (as if this were a rudimentary precaution), "if I tell you I am coming from Munich, then really I will come from Vienna"—but then Savo did not strike him as particularly bright. On the train, Michel said, Savo hid his painting in the place where chumps always hid their goods—behind a ceiling panel over a toilet—and there two of Michel's people, disguised as customs officials, found it and confiscated it. The painting wasn't Savo's—it apparently belonged to a bigger cheese—and Savo, terrified of going back to the owner empty-handed, came to Michel as a supplicant. "I gave him back the piece," Michel said, "but I made him sweat first."

We had left the park by now and had arrived in front of a little restaurant named De Haagsche Traiteur; we seated ourselves upstairs beside a window looking down over a narrow street with an art gallery and a china shop. Michel talked and laughed with the owner, who vanished for a moment and returned bearing bowls of lobster bisque. When we had finished the soup, I said to Michel, "Do you know who has the missing mosaics?"

"Absolutely," he replied. "Aydin has them. Savo's fronting for him, but Aydin has them. Aydin has many storages, in the most funny parts of Munich—places where you would never expect him to have millions and millions of dollars' worth of pieces: little apartments, et cetera. He builds fake walls, which is fantastically clever, so if you are in one of the apartments you will never expect that there are treasures."

I asked Michel if he knew how Yanni Petsopoulos had managed to arrange the return of the two Kanakariá mosaics—Saints Jude and Bartholomew —to Cyprus in 1984. His reply took me back to the baffling events surrounding the Menil Foundation's purchase of the Lysi frescoes from Aydin Dikmen. The foundation had put the money for Dikmen in an escrow account, Michel related, "and then, you see, Petsopoulos said, 'The money's in the account, and you can get it whenever Cyprus and the Menil start to feel comfortable. And for them to feel comfortable, I'd like to have from you the mosaics, and I will hand the mosaics to the right people in the right place.' Well, Aydin, he's crazy for money—oh, oh, this one million dollars in his escrow account!" And so, Michel said, Petsopoulos had "pressed" Dikmen to deliver the mosaics into the custody of Constantine Leventis. "But Aydin, not being an idiot, kept the good pieces—including the Feet of Christ, which is now here in Holland with the Yugoslavs."

"Oh, so Marko and Draža still have the Feet?"

In a flash Michel's face turned steely and cold, and he fixed me with a hostile glare. Nothing remained of his usual affability. "These names are not so easy to remember," he said, in a menacing tone, "especially for you, an American. I mentioned them only once, a few minutes ago. I think you know them, you have heard them before. Tell me: where, and from whom?"

Suddenly I understood that I had threatened Michel, that I had trespassed unwittingly against him. Considering the Yugoslavs to be merely another potential source of information, I had forgotten that they were actors, maybe principals, in the drama. I did not know their real motives, to whom they answered, or to what lengths they would go, yet in attempting to reach them by phone, I was straying into the camp of Michel's sworn enemies. My mind raced, searching for a way to allay his suspicions, and looking him straight in the eye, I said, "Those names came up in Indianapolis, at the trial—they figured in several depositions"—which was not exactly correct, which was even a little untrue, since nobody at the trial had named those names, they hadn't been mentioned at all, and yet . . . the notion was certainly plausible; it was believable enough to satisfy Michel, and indeed his features at once rearranged themselves into their normal look of confidentiality.

"Unfortunately, the Marko and Draža group still have the Feet," he said, resuming his tale. "Savo makes himself a little presentable, but if you see Marko and Draža, they are not presentable, they're really absolutely—" Michel made a gesture of dismissal. "They *cannot* deal, so I'm sure they will try to find a way for Savo to sell the Feet. But it's a pity, because the pieces should all be reunited. Cyprus cannot officially make them an offer, because if, as a government, Cyprus starts dealing, where is the end?"

All this time, Michel's portable phone had been lying beside him on the windowsill. Now it began to buzz, and he clicked it on. At first, there seemed to be some trouble on the line, but then Michel's face took on a radiant expression. "Bob!" he exclaimed. "How are you?" He winked at me and jerked up his eyebrows; I realized that he was talking to Bob Fitzgerald. "I'm sitting with some people," Michel said—that apparently meant me—"but I can talk for a moment."

They chatted enthusiastically about several deals—there was mention of a Cézanne watercolor—and then Michel hung up, flushed with excitement. He ordered fish for us and recounted some practical jokes he had once played on Bob. "I love it when I outsmart him," he said. "That is the fight always between us. I mean, we love each other, but we fight each other from the moment I am in business with him. When I've *got* him, I really enjoy it, and he must be something like a sadomasochist, because he loves it also—because he accepts and respects it."

"Bob likes to talk about his great losses as well as his great victories," I said.

"Yes, well, we've lost lots of money and we've made lots of money," said Michel, his voice dwindling awkwardly. All at once, his face suffered a galvanic change of expression, from cheerfully roguish to troubled, almost anguished. "I don't know when you spoke to him," he said. "If it was when I was fighting with him—" He broke off, pained, I supposed, by the memory of the fistfight Bob had told me about, and the mutually inflicted black eyes. "Well, I won't ask you what he says about me, because I know what he thinks."

"He's annoyed at you," I said. "At least, he was a month ago."

Ever since I had started to follow the mosaics affair, I found that I was listening to people talk about money: prices, markups, commissions, contingency fees. Each time lucre changed hands, there was a shift of psychic position, a scramble for dominance, but in the telling the numbers grew sad and the details lost their glitter. Now I leaned forward and looked hopefully at Michel, thinking that he was going to talk to me about something else—about his great friendship with Bob, an attachment that was apparently composed of equal parts sibling struggle and boyish rascality. But Michel averted his gaze and made a huddle of his fingers on the table. When, at length, I engaged his attention, he began speaking of something else. He did not again touch upon his friendship with Bob, and when the time came for me to say goodbye to him, it was this omission that I regretted the most.

On my last evening in The Hague, Michel and I stood outside De Haagsche Traiteur while the light faded and a frail moon rose and the sidewalk filled up with people. They waved to each other and then gathered in knots, and some women giggled vivaciously, overloudly; the people were like an opera chorus gathering for a street scene, a big *tutti*. I remarked at the people, at their elegance.

"It's just a little party I am throwing," said Michel. "For you, to say goodbye."

"For me?"

"It's a very small party, you understand. The best I could do at such short notice!" He flung his arm around my shoulder.

There came a noise like a locomotive whistle and a

foghorn and snare drum rolled into one, and a melody started up, all the sounds chugging together, and from around the corner strode a man trundling a huge street organ. Then somebody popped champagne, and the party was on.

We drank the champagne and listened to the street organ. On its front side were four carved figures in gumdrop colors: a blond woman, a clown, a crook, a constable. They stood stockstill—they did not nod or march stiffly about—but if you went behind the organ to where the organ-grinder was standing, you could watch cogwheels turning, belts spinning, and mechanical arms striking cymbals and drums. Michel was transfixed by the music, and when it was over he told me a beautiful story about the street organs, their music arrangers and designers and carvers, and about how he had tried to revive the patronage of this fine old Dutch tradition.

After the organ had finished its concert, we went upstairs in De Haagsche Traiteur and ate matjes herring and a great steamed salmon. We sang "Amsterdam, Amsterdam," which the organ had just been playing.

"Did you like the organ?" asked a delicate girl standing beside me.

"Marvelous," I replied dutifully.

"No, it is not marvelous, it is horrible," she said. "Always when I try to sleep he comes up under my window, the gypsy, and begins that sound, that nightmarish sound—" But more music swelled and drowned out her voice, because Henri Cordino, a famous accordionist, had just arrived and he had taken up his famous accordion, which Michel said was a work of art, and was playing every Tin Pan Alley song he could think of. He stood with his weight on one foot and his head thrown back and played without stopping, on and on; after a while somebody told him to lay aside his instrument and eat, but Michel said, laughing, that Henri was a gypsy and would never turn his back on anything he owned.

"*Ik ben een smokkelaer,*" sang the people.

I am a smuggler, in the dark
Of night I bring my loot across the border.

They came from every walk of life: a stunt man, a dentist, a graying lawyer who kicked up his heels and did the kazatsky. All the women were lovely.

They asked Henri Cordino to take suggestions, and he played all their favorite tunes for them: show tunes, folk tunes, top forty tunes—there was no tune Henri did not know. His head was startlingly small and ruggedly chiseled, like a lion's head carved in the arm-rest of a chair, and he smiled cryptically back at the people and played their tunes without ever saying what he liked or hated, or what he would have played if he were back home with the gypsies. On and on he played, perhaps for two hours, and then came a sudden discordance, a confusion of keys, and I looked over and saw that Michel was standing beside him singing a strange song, a song that Henri Cordino could not guess how to play.

"*Mein Yiddishe Mamme,*" sang Michel, inexplicably. He was glaring at me with that angry, pixilated expression he got when he'd been drinking. Did he know about my failed attempt to contact his former bodyguards? He stopped singing and came over.

Still training his bare eye on me—the eye not hidden by his shock of hair—he contemplated me with disgust. "You know, if you'd been anyone special," he said, "I would have invited the mayor!"

"I like these people," I said. "And I don't like mayors."

His eye burned a path to my brain, and then he let out a burst of laughter.

"You and I, we're going to fight each other," he cried jovially. "It's good, we make a big fight!" He clapped the nape of my neck with his hand and held out the other for a handshake. "Yes! It is good between us. I'm sorry I didn't invite more important people, perhaps the director of the Mauritshuis." Then his voice fell away, tangled in Henri Cordino's chords, and he danced bearishly off, singing *"Mein Yiddishe Mamme."*

I had one final day in Holland, a day to dry out, and just before I was to leave Amsterdam I found myself walking on Anna Vondelstraat, not far from the Marriott Hotel where Peg Goldberg had first met Michel van Rijn; on an impulse I continued as far as the hotel itself. The sidewalk café was still there, and so were the ancient plane trees, the copper beech, the herring and fruit stands, the great neo-Gothic gable of the American Hotel with its clock tower telling the time. A large sign outside the Marriott said BYZANTIUM and pointed toward a new shopping complex bearing that name. I wanted to question these mute things, to ask what they knew about two saints and an archangel and a divine child who had passed this way two years before; but they stared disdainfully back at me, partners in a conspiracy of silence.

Still following the same impulse, I crossed four or five humpbacked bridges until I came to an avenue busy with fast-food hangouts and penny arcades, and as I continued walking I heard the brilliant piping of a street organ; it was worked by a giant of a gypsy who beat time with a cupful of coins, eyes staring into vacancy. I stopped, and became aware that I was standing in front of an ancient and rather shabby-looking house whose four stories were capped by a gable with two whimsical volutes. Recognizing the house from Peg's description, I rang and was buzzed in.

"Mr. Vecht?"

A white-haired gentleman bobbed toward me down a staircase of three steps; his green-and-russet tweed suit made a pointillist blur amid the vitrines and tapestry chairs. He halted and scrutinized me with a look of resignation.

"Ah, the press. I suppose it was inevitable."

"I'd like to know about the Modigliani," I said, introducing myself.

"I understand."

We seated ourselves on the tapestry chairs, beside a case full of Chinese objets de vertu. He gave a wry smile and adjusted his horn-rimmed glasses; warily his eyes engaged mine.

"The Modigliani I did not really wish to sell," he began. "My father bought it in 1919, from the artist himself, in the Café du Dôme. I inherited it. She saw it hanging, but she did not seriously inspect it."

"What about Bob Fitzgerald?"

"You know, I thought he was working for *her*. He told me he likes to go to Germany to buy Porsches to resell in Japan." Vecht smiled at the ceiling and waggled his head. "Some *fantaisie*, eh?"

I nodded. I'd been aware that Bob sold vintage cars but not that he made buying trips to Germany.

"If only she had come to me," Vecht said, sighing. "If only she had asked my advice. I am the fifth generation in this shop. Of course, I know Michel. I know the father, terribly nice. Michel, too, is a nice boy—but be careful! A good friend of his was in prison for something, I think maybe taxes. Michel is always coming with Rolls-Royces, suites in five-star hotels. I'm not impressed."

I said, "I'd like to see your Modigliani," and, not wishing to put Vecht on the spot, turned to examine a Barbizon landscape on the wall. Then I looked back at him. He was staring at me in disbelief; smiling, he glanced parenthetically to one side, as if sharing his incredulity with an invisible colleague.

"*Then* I had it," he replied. "Now? I don't tell you!"

By mid-1991, Savo Kujundzic was apparently spending a lot of time at a new suite of offices he had opened in Vienna for his small engineering firm. Now and then I would ring his number and ask for Mr. Kujundzic, but my request was always met with a leisurely stream of Russian, a language I do not understand. It was my invariable impression that I was being mistaken for someone else, and only after I insisted that I knew no Russian would the voice, which was affable and male, pursue its explanations in English. This English, refined but hesitant, was heavily accented, as if learned by a person who, though very keen to know the language, had never lived anyplace where it is spoken. "Savwo is not khere," the voice would say, and then volunteer the news that he was away in Belgrade or Munich or Moscow. "I know nothing of this question you khave for Savwo, but I know that he is expyecting you."

In England on unrelated business one afternoon that summer—it was a few weeks after I'd first called Savo's office—I impulsively hopped a plane to Vienna, caught a cab into the city, and took a room opposite the Staatsoper. Dusk was falling over the linden alleys and the flickering streetcars and the hurrying people in their opera clothes. In the lingering blue light I sat down in the embrasure of the window and phoned Savo's firm, G. & R. Handelsgesellschaft. A brisk, efficient-sounding woman answered, and told me in good English to hold the line. I caught a gabbling sound, as if multitudes were conversing in the background. After a longish moment, a surprisingly friendly voice greeted me: Savo's tone had the Montenegrin forthrightness, with its hint of bravado, and also the Montenegrin nasality—an unexpected timbre for so deep a voice. In a few words he informed me that he was busy, that his offices were filled with the members of a Russian trade delegation, and that he would call back in an hour or so; then we could meet and talk and perhaps share a meal. He hung up. Two hours passed, and it grew dark, but still Savo did not call, and I rang his number again. This time he himself answered, and he told me that he was still tied up with the visiting Russians—but he would try to call the next day or perhaps the day after.

The following morning I was awakened from a deep sleep by the trilling of the phone: it was Savo, who summoned me to an address near the Südbahnhof. I caught a cab, which headed south until it was crawling through a maze of mean streets fronted by long, barracks-like buildings of the sort that commonly house dispatch offices, transshipment agencies, freight-insurance brokers—all the bewildering bureaucracy of goods transportation. Not a soul was in sight. At length, the cab stopped before a large frosted-glass door, beside which was an embossed plaque bearing the name of Savo's company. I stepped out into the heavy, almost breathable silence of the street and rang the doorbell.

As I stood waiting for the door to open, some phrases from the sworn statement Savo had made to Peg's lawyer in Indianapolis the year before drifted back into my mind. He had spoken of Aydin Dikmen's horror and distress at the "fairy tale" told by Yanni Petsopoulos and retold by Walter Hopps in his pretrial deposition of May 1989; upon learning of this testimony, Dikmen had raged against Hopps in his Munich apartment, cursing him as "miserable Popps." Whatever Petsopoulos or Hopps might say, he had never had any mosaic roundel hanging over his red sofa, and nobody had ever smashed a decanter in his fireplace.

Savo, too, had declared himself appalled by this story. "Petsopoulos can tell this to his mother," he'd said. Savo had also testified that during trips he made on Peg's behalf, in May 1990, to Istanbul and to northern Cyprus, he had met with two men, the trader Ahmet Aziz—the same that Dikmen had praised to Peg—and a certain Mehmet, who had verified with documents the extent of Cypriot officialdom's collusion with Dikmen. The remarkable thing about Savo was that he, unlike all the others, wished, as he had put it, "to help the lady." But why? Why did he wish to help her? There were so many whys in this affair.

The person who opened the door to me was a smiling woman of middle age who introduced herself as Maria and led me upstairs to a large, bare office with walls of roughcast plaster. There were, I noticed, no drafting tables or engineer's instruments. At the far side of a long, empty table sat a man with a squarish face and dark eyes, who puffed furiously on a cigarette. The eyes were wistful and a little evasive. "Hello, I am Grisha," he said.

I introduced myself and asked where he was from.

"I am from Moscow," he said, puffing. I recognized his voice as that of the man who usually answered the phone; Maria was clearly the efficient-sounding woman I had spoken to the day before.

Maria said, "Would you like some coffee?"

Grisha and I replied yes in unison, and Maria gave us a dry look and said, "I perform here many functions, from the highest to the lowest."

She went to get the coffee and returned. "Milk?" We said yes.

"I am here always the mother, never the child," said Maria, and then added, glancing at me, "I do not know anything of why you have come."

"I also do not know," said Grisha.

And then as I stirred my coffee I became aware that a very large man was standing in front of me, holding out a very large hand. Savo's hair was thick and black; his eyes peered from under dense, nearly meeting eyebrows; and his jutting jaw and somewhat skewed nose, which gave his face the look of being slightly pushed in at the center, inevitably suggested a boxer. He was casually dressed, in slacks and a polo shirt, but his stance was vaguely military. His demeanor, as he showed me into an adjoining office, disclosed no anxiety about the implications of our meeting. He seemed a product of centuries of martial breeding, and only some interesting quirk of character, I felt, could have landed him in this office beside a railroad and not in the mountains of his South Slav homeland.

Besides his native Serbian, Savo spoke fluent Russian and German and some French; he had also taught himself a rudimentary English, which he regarded as undependable. As for me, I understand German fairly well but do not speak it. For these reasons, Savo decided to use German and I to use English, while Maria would stand by as interpreter, ready to elucidate any phrase that might puzzle either one of us. We sat down opposite each other.

It was important, he began, with a look of weary contempt playing across his face, to understand the Cypriot cast of mind and, above all, to understand the Cypriot involvement with shadow plays. The Greeks had invented this art form in ancient times, and they had been living in their shadow-play world for many centuries. If at one time they had had a great culture, now all that culture was gone—gone except for "the shadow plays—the shadow plays and the lies."

I began to object to this generalization, but Savo swept away my words with a peremptory gesture. He could not understand, he said, why no American official could grasp what "every bird in Europe" knew: that nobody wanted to tell the whole truth about the Kanakariá affair because nobody wanted to be enmeshed in it. This, he insisted, was especially true of Dominique de Menil and Walter Hopps, because of the peculiar manner in which they had acquired the

Lysi frescoes. As for Dr. Karageorghis, the reason he hadn't come to testify in Indianapolis, Savo said, was that between 1964 and 1974, when the Turkish Cypriots had withdrawn into fortified enclaves, he had commissioned Aydin Dikmen to go around photographing Byzantine churches inaccessible to the Greek Cypriot authorities. Karageorghis could deny this if he wished (I was certain that he would), but Savo insisted that "everybody in Cyprus" knew that it was true.

As for Yanni Petsopoulos, he had done a measure of business with Dikmen and had taken many things on consignment from him to sell in London. Savo reiterated something he had said in his sworn statement in Indianapolis: that after the trial, in August or September 1989, he had recovered from Petsopoulos a number of antiquities that Dikmen had left with him. So what was all the nonsense about Petsopoulos's "rescuing" Cypriot art from Dikmen? They did business with each other all the time!

Though I didn't know Petsopoulos, I was sure he would dispute this contention. For the moment, however, I merely took notes, glancing at Maria whenever I was uncertain of the meaning of some German expression. She was sitting beside me, scribbling on a pad; I could see her in my peripheral vision—a blur of red lipstick and a flutter of glossy red hair. Her expression was that of a person detained on meaningless business.

Then Savo began to explain how he had come to be involved in this intrigue. He claimed that he had no monetary interest at stake, that his actions were based purely on his friendship with Dikmen. Dikmen was anguished, he said; he felt that he could not help himself by anything he might say in a courtroom. He was not a self-confident man, and he was also a Turk, with the Turkish secretiveness, but if he had come to the trial, he could have destroyed the Cypriot case against Peg Goldberg in five minutes.

Savo's tone was even, matter-of-fact, grenade-launcher-manual, as if he hadn't the slightest doubt of the truth of what he was saying, or much interest, really, in what I might make of it. He stopped to light a cigarette, and pressed on.

He said that two men he had known since childhood, two bodyguards named Marko and Draža, had told him that Michel had artfully persuaded them, together with a Dutchman called Hans, to lend him money against the sale of the Hand of Mary and Feet of Christ, promising each of them $250,000 in return—although it would take a little while, Michel had pointed out, for the sale to go through. "Michel had no money," Savo said. "He just eats up money, so he borrowed from Marko, Draža, and Hans—the poor kids were actually *supporting* him."

It was very peculiar, I thought, the way all these errant lives led back to each other in the end, like balls in a pinball machine. "Savo, how can it be that your two childhood friends Marko and Draža just *happened* to wind up as Michel's bodyguards?" I asked. "Isn't that a pretty odd coincidence?"

Savo seemed not to understand my question, for he didn't answer it.

"Savo," said Maria in German, "what this man wants to know is how, out of all the Yugoslavs in the world, you happened to know these two—the bodyguards of this person called Michel."

Now Savo understood, and he nodded gravely.

"Marko and Draža are Montenegrins," he said in English, throwing me a level glance. "Montenegro is small country. To Europe come wery few Montenegrins. Every Montenegrin man know every other Montenegrin man."

I said, "What are Marko's and Draža's last names—their surnames? Do you know?"

He laughed, but there was severity in his laughter. "They are not like you and me," he said. "They live in different world, primitive world. No last names."

There came a knock at the door, and Savo was temporarily called away. I seized the opportunity to talk to Maria. "Where are you from, Maria, originally?" I asked.

"From many countries, from everywhere," she replied, a little sadly, "although now I am Viennese."

"And what is your position in this firm?"

"I am an engineering consultant," she said, handing me a business card that read "Maria Salzmann, Konsulentin."

"What field of engineering do you specialize in?" I persisted, feeling that, one way or another, her reply was sure to disclose something interesting about Savo's occupation.

"Avalanche forecasting," she said offhandedly.

Savo re-entered the room, smiling broadly at us—a generous, Mediterranean smile. He obviously didn't care if I had quizzed Maria; he didn't care what Maria told me. He sat down in his chair, leaning way back, and his eyes shone brightly.

Then he started to tell me about Aydin Dikmen—something about a rich Istanbul family, large inherited properties, a passion for historic preservation, the restoration of whole districts of the city. Besides a museumlike villa outside the Turkish city of Konya, he said, Dikmen had acres of space in Munich, but was attached to his small flat on the Schützenstrasse, which his wife and child also preferred. I had to understand that that *Schwein* Michel had blown poor Dikmen's cover. When Peg Goldberg refused to give Michel control over the marketing of the mosaics, Michel had gone to the press out of pique: he had summoned Geraldine Norman of *The Independent* to The Hague and had shown her an old option agreement signed by Dikmen. This document proved that Dikmen had possessed the four Kanakariá mosaics sold in 1988 to Peg. Another problem, Savo said, was Dikmen's name on the fully executed bill of sale to Peg, which he had foolishly signed when it was half blank, before the price and the name of the buyer had been filled in.

"Savo, hold on," I protested, put off by what seemed a chain of melodramatic plot devices. "Do you mean to tell me that your friend Aydin Dikmen actually signed a contract that was only partly completed?"

"Yes, absolutely," said Savo. He insisted that Dikmen had believed all along that the mosaics would go to Constantine Leventis—just as had happened in 1984—and, through him, back to Cyprus; Dikmen and Leventis had already discussed this once, in Frankfurt, but hadn't agreed on the price, Savo said. At that time Dikmen had asked 90,000 Deutsche marks—or about $45,000—per piece, which Leventis wouldn't pay, so when van Rijn waved $350,000 in his face for four pieces he accepted the offer. And no, Dikmen had never seen the bill of sale as it was finally drawn up; he had signed it before it showed the name of the buyer or the price, and it was written in a language, English, that he could not read.

Savo conveyed a striking impression of loyalty to Aydin Dikmen. Coming himself from a land governed by unwritten rules, by eternal blood ties and fierce oaths of fealty, he seemed intensely indignant over the way in which his friend had been treated. At the same time, I sensed that this meeting of ours had its own, independent emotional weight: it was a context in which Savo could assert his native gregariousness, his willingness to give all comers the benefit of the doubt. Subject to the natural anxieties of the Balkan émigré in a Germanic environment, he was broadening his circle of acquaintances.

Now Savo began to try out more of his own English, like somebody secretly eager to practice it, and soon he was speaking it exclusively. "You must understand that Aydin is one wery good man," he said. "He trust his friends, and Michel play on that trust. They do business for six, seven years and no problems. Michel was often in Munich, he have own apartment near the Englischer Garten, and he buy every good icon that come into the city. Then he send this blank bill of sale to Aydin in Geneva, and get a friend to pretend to be Aydin and shake hands with Peg. A little later, a quarrel start between Aydin and Michel over the blank bill of sale, and Michel say that if Aydin signed it he was stupid, just stupid."

Savo's face lost its lively expression, and a dark thought shadowed his brow. Something like a snort escaped him. "Michel will not live long," he said.

I looked up from my notepad. "Why not?"

"Some people—"

"Yugoslavs?"

"No, not Yugoslavs. Others. They are looking for him."

"What others?"

"Ah, this does not concern you. Michel have many enemies."

Something gilded or golden had been glimmering all the while on a corner of Savo's desk. I leaned forward and looked at it closely. It was an expensive reproduction of an icon of the Blessed Virgin.

"Savo," I said, "are you an Orthodox Christian, a believer?"

"Yes, of course," he replied, without hesitation.

And now I recalled that in Savo's sworn statement, when Joe Emerson had asked him if he knew where the remaining mosaics were, he had answered, a bit uncomfortably, that he did.

"Savo," I said, as calmly as I could, "do *you* have the missing mosaics?"

"You may say I have some share in them," he replied evasively.

"Well, if you have some share in them," I went on, "how can you possibly claim to have no financial stake in the outcome of this affair?"

I saw that Maria's eyes held the same question, and I assumed that it would unsettle Savo: his admission of some kind of ownership seemed compromising, since the Kanakariá mosaics had been established by an American court to be Cypriot Church property. But his features retained their accustomed geniality. "Okay, I have a stake," he replied. "But that is not the principal thing. The principal thing is my friendship to Aydin."

· 137 ·

"Did Aydin sell you your interest?" I asked.

"No, some Turkish Cypriots did. But tell me," he added, with a fleeting frown, "why are the Greeks so concerned about these mosaics? I know where are hundreds of Cypriot treasures. I have offered to tell them, to make a trade, but they never answered me. They are not interested. I know where is something much more waluable than these mosaics—something wery important to every Cypriot Christian."

"What is that?"

"The Mummy of Saint Lazarus," he said.

I was dumbfounded. I knew that Lazarus had been expelled from Bethany after his resurrection by Jesus, then forced into exile on an unseaworthy vessel which brought him as far as Citium, in Cyprus—today the port of Larnaca. There he was found by the apostles, consecrated a bishop, and after his death canonized. But his mortal remains had been removed from Citium in A.D. 890, and his sarcophagus, which still stands in a church that bears his name, had been empty for more than a thousand years. If Savo knew where the relic of Lazarus had been spirited, he knew something very remarkable indeed.

"Are you sure you don't mean somebody else?" I asked weakly. "Maybe, oh, Saint Barnabas? Or Saint Mamas?"

"No!" he said firmly. "The Mummy of Saint Lazarus."

Our meeting had obviously drawn to a conclusion. We agreed to meet again before long, and Maria escorted me out. In front of the building, I asked her what project the firm was currently working on.

"We are trying to buy something for a Soviet en-

terprise," she answered. "A system for keeping pack-
aged cement wet."

"I see," I replied, and then, pointing at the embossed logo on the wall, I said, "Tell me, Maria, what
does this stand for—this G. & R. Handelsgesellschaft?"

"I really have no idea," she replied.

5

Savo promised to do his best to bundle Aydin Dikmen over from Munich, so I moved into a cheap hotel, a place to wait in, and telephoned him at regular intervals to ask when Dikmen was coming.

He said, "Maybe after two days."

He said, "Over the weekend."

He said, "One day more."

"Why don't I just go to Munich and talk to him there?"

"No, he is Turkish man, many secrets, hides everything. No *Selbstvertrauen*."

"Self-confidence?"

"*Ja.* Maybe with me, in Wien or Tschechoslowakei, he is more open, more joking, but in München never. In München, he have one boss, and that is his wife, Koca. Koca never let Aydin talk. Wait here in Wien. I bring him, I try."

Out on the streets, the sun beat down, and the rippling Jugendstil palaces rippled with especial vivacity in the broiling air. The Viennese weren't sure how to handle the greenhouse effect; they mopped their brows frantically, and their glasses slipped on their noses. I wandered around, theoretically waiting for Dikmen but only half believing in his existence. Not that there wasn't a man by that name, a Turk who was living in Munich; but he filled too many roles, had too many skills—he was a logically impossible person. I reasoned that the real Dikmen could not be anything but a half-pint version of the Dikmen of legend. Even this person (granting that he wasn't purely fictitious) seemed to be dodging everyone now, and he certainly seemed wary of me. What assurance did the poor fellow have, after all, that I really was a writer and not an agent for some political faction or commercial entity? His recalcitrance was understandable. Did I grasp the real motives of those to whom I talked? Take Savo, for instance: was he keeping Dikmen under "house arrest," as, a year and a half earlier, the elegant gentleman calling himself Dikmen had told Peg's interpreter in Amsterdam; or was he "fronting" for him, as Michel van Rijn had suggested to me a few weeks ago; or was he something quite different—maybe a Russian agent who freelanced in the antiquities trade? Or, then again, was he just what he said he was—an honest émigré engineer? All I knew was that I was stranded in Vienna, with very little to do.

Standing in an ice-cream line I met an elderly Italian and his even more elderly mother, and they invited me to accompany them to a nearby park behind a palace. Despite the weather both wore raincoats and carried umbrellas, and the man had a rain hat pulled down firmly over his ears. Following an alley of plane trees, we came at length to a colossal pile of masonry—a broken arch spanning a pool—which the Italian regarded with an air of amusement. It was, he said, a make-believe ruin, erected in the eighteenth century by a very important Austrian family called Asburgo, which liked to stress its connection to the past. As he stood there, gesturing at the ruin, I saw that he carried a scholarly guidebook to Vienna, and I also saw that he and his mother had been wise to wear raincoats, because the sky was gradually darkening and a rush of cool air had suddenly ballooned our clothes. Afraid of taking a chill, the pair inspected the droplets of rain on their sleeves and put up their umbrellas; then they bade me a polite farewell and hurried back down the alley of trees until they vanished in a green turning.

It began to rain, furiously at first, then more fitfully. I took shelter under a tree and looked down at the stone lip of the pool. It was composed, rather disjointedly, of pieces of cornice obviously removed from some other site, for kindred fragments cropped up out of the greenish water in planned disorder. The ruin, a studied reminder of the course of empire and the doom of princes, was an Italianate "capriccio" graced with many of the genre's regulation features: soffit encrusted with broken rosettes; frieze of angry maenads with masks and drinking bowls; sculpted vine leaves reaching down toward the water; and, at the center of the pool, river god and nymph rising out of a shivering reflection of themselves. As I scrutinized the thing, I remembered that it was common in the chatter of antiquities shops to speak of the antique as having once been modern, to speak of motifs like egg-and-dart or ailanthus as having been on the cutting edge of design; but like so many urns and fauns and pipes of Pan, oddments in the vitrines lining the walls of those cluttered shops, this nice old folly had never expressed any fresh feeling or thought. Back and back you could travel in time, how far you scarcely even knew, before you encountered the originals of these formal conventions, and if every generation found a propitious moment to revive them, that was largely because they carried the taint of an eternally amusing falseness and theatricality.

Well, now we, in the late twentieth century, were living through our own revival of the antique, and just as in the marketplace for contemporary art, most of the pieces fobbed off as masterpieces were really of the most dubious aesthetic value. Perhaps the best pieces in the best shops were genuinely expressive, but the rest could only be prized, as the case might be, for rarity, religious interest, the use of precious metals, showy splendor, or just because they filled in the lacunae in a "set" of something or other. The trade in such objects was a dream mill, spinning out chimeras irresistible to a certain passive need for self-deception, a kind of hypnotic suggestibility. Ironically, the quest for the ancient, the authentic, the rooted, the hallowed, seemed to call forth particularly dubious or shifty stratagems, and even the most respectable dealers, collectors, and curators depended on a class of audacious brokers—people not chary of doing business with tomb robbers and church burglars—from whom they hypocritically averted their eyes. Against all reason, the dealers and collectors and curators seemed to feel that if they handled "noble" objects long enough, the nobility would somehow rub off on them.

My thoughts returned to the ruin before me. It was

really a stage set, and a wonderful one at that. I studied the ridiculous maenads, the ringleted heroes: they were invincibly voguish, exempt from the verdicts of taste. Whatever its original function, the ruin no longer advertised anything but itself, and though it had once been a fake antique, it was now quite real in its way. The illusion was created and dispelled in one twinkling of an eye, and that, no doubt, was the source of its appeal. Deception had this built-in irony, that in order to enjoy it you had to know that it had happened, and if you yourself were the dissembler, you would feel bound to unmask yourself in the end. Artistry craves recognition—this holds as true for the hot-air artist as for any other. It occurred to me that those who had floated so many bubbles of mendacity about the Kanakariá mosaics would probably be quite happy to burst them, for the sheer joy of parading their powers of deceit.

The rain had now ceased; the pool had regained its glassy surface and mineral-green tone. Up above, the clouds had come apart, and parallel shafts of sunlight streamed down through the trees. The birdsong, which had died away, resumed, and I saw that in the pool, beside the bulrushes surrounding the god and nymph, a mallard had settled, his emerald breast as shiny and artificial-looking as a patch of Day-Glo paint. He ruffled his feathers and cocked a skeptical eye at me, and I recalled Savo's odd remark that "every bird in Europe" knew more about the mosaics case than the most informed of my compatriots. There certainly was a great deal that I did not understand, and I hastened back to my hotel to review once again my ever-growing pile of notepads and documents.

By late spring of 1991, Peg, who was still in Indianapolis, had managed to develop a certain rapport with Ahmet Aziz and Mehmet, the Turkish Cypriots whom she had first heard about when Savo mentioned them in his sworn statement and who kept popping up in almost everyone's account of what had gone on. (She thought she'd met Mehmet when she encountered Dikmen in Amsterdam, in the fall of 1989, but she had never once seen Ahmet.) The two claimed, among other things, that they had proof that Vassos Karageorghis had long engaged in practices that violated Cypriot law; it was rumored that Ahmet, whose family had known Karageorghis for many years before the Turkish invasion in 1974, had himself been granted unusual dispensations by Karageorghis but had fallen from favor as a result of his own rather too enterprising approach to commerce. Whether or not this was true, he evidently nursed a certain hostility toward Karageorghis.

Peg, for her part, wanted to obtain legally admissible evidence that Cypriot officials had long colluded with Aydin Dikmen. In late February 1991, immediately after the Supreme Court denied her request for an appeal, she had placed a transatlantic call to Ahmet, in northern Cyprus. He saluted her amiably and chatted with her awhile: his gravelly voice and beguiling accent—half Turkish, half London—conjured up the image of a tough yet openhearted man in late middle life. She explained to him that she wanted to get an injunction against the removal of the mosaics from the United States and that, according to her understanding of the law, this would require her to produce fresh evidence. Could he help her prove, for example, that Greek Cypriot officials had permitted residents of the island to acquire important Christian antiquities?

He replied that he did in fact possess evidence of such misconduct.

"And you can actually prove it?" she asked.

"Absolutely. I can prove it with names as well."

"And items that they sold?"

"Well"—he sounded put off—"I don't know about Aydin."

"No, no. *Items*," she said, enunciating precisely. "Pieces—that they sold."

But apparently Ahmet was still thinking about Aydin Dikmen. "I arranged a meeting between Aydin and Karageorghis," he said. "Or other officials. Yes, I can prove that as well."

"You can prove that you arranged meetings between Aydin and Karageorghis?" she asked, delighted.

"Of course. There are many things I can prove. Many things. And with names and dates. And these are officials, either with the United Nations—okay?—or diplomats, because these were the people who could cross the border during that time. Nobody else could cross the border. That is why, for example, Karageorghis used to send diplomats here—'Go and do this for me'—and he used to pay money. What *happened* to those pieces that they were taking from the churches in the Turkish quarter? He can't *show* them, can he?"

"And you can prove that you were present at meetings when Karageorghis and Dikmen were doing business?"

"Of course. Only there is one problem."

"What?"

"The problem is, I got in touch with Aydin last week. He wants a written statement from you that he never met you in 1988 and he never sold you the mosaics. And this, as far as I know, you promised him in Germany."

"I gave him one copy, and he tore it up," Peg said.

"Now he wants that paper," Ahmet said heatedly. "If you give that paper to him, I promise you we are going to solve this problem."

She said, "I even told Aydin when I went to Germany that in order to help him I would be willing to go to Turkey to testify that he was not the man I met in Switzerland—that van Rijn substituted somebody."

This seemed to suit Ahmet. "He is going to help us," he said. "Because, now *I'm* in this business, he hasn't got any other choice. I'll tell you the truth. He knows that what I tell, it will be against him. He offered me some money, and I didn't accept, because I wanted to be on your side."

When I heard this conversation on tape—Peg was playing it for an audience of curious people during one of my brief visits to Indianapolis—I strained to make out these last phrases. What, I wondered, did Ahmet have to "tell," and why had Dikmen offered him money? Why was Ahmet on Peg's side now? Listening intently, I could hear Peg's sighs on the tape, and sense her terrible frustration.

Further along in the conversation, Peg told Ahmet, "The idiot Cypriots are probably going to put the mosaics on display at the Indianapolis Museum of Art, in order to make me look that much worse in my own hometown. So if they do that—if Noland lets them have them next week—and we can file a lawsuit fast enough, then we have a chance to seize them again, so they don't get out of this country." She emphasized her need for documentary proof of Cypriot perjury. "We need to be able to prove that Leventis and Karageorghis and Dikmen and Petsopoulos were doing face-to-face business all along," she said.

"Yes, we are going to prove that," he said. "No problem for us. Trust me. No problem."

For a few moments they discussed a future exchange of faxes. Then Ahmet said, "When a new ambassador comes here, from any country, they give him valuable antiquities as a present—which they shouldn't do. They have to keep the pieces in the museums, instead of giving them away."

"So it's only different for me," Peg said, her voice thick with hurt.

"Yes," he said. "We all know their games." And then, sounding rather embarrassed, he began mumbling something about his financial situation. "I don't want to ask money from Aydin, because I don't want to be on his side," he said. "But if I'm going to be on *your* side, you have to look after me. I mean, if I had enough money, I wouldn't ask at all." He was beginning to sound pressured and uneasy. Did he think he might have to leave Cyprus and set up shop elsewhere, out of reach of some enemy or enemies?

"I will do everything possible, everything I can," Peg said, her despair almost palpable now.

"Trust me," he pleaded.

"Okay," she said.

"In the end, you will see what sort of person I am," he said.

She said, "I sure hope it's a good person."

"Of course."

"I've had enough experience with bad persons," she said.

"Eat slowly," Savo told me. "German food is heavy, make you sick."

A sheepdog flounced by, followed by five giggling children.

"Is funny," Savo said, knitting his brow. "Germans cannot do simple things like cook food, but do difficult things wery well. German colonial policy wery effective toward Slav people." He gnawed the meat off a rib as the sheepdog circled back, faster this time, the tots shrieking. Then he palmed another rib. "Slovenia is German plot," he said. "Why do you think there is fighting for customs houses on Austrian border?"

"You tell me," I said.

"German guns," said Savo. "Hey, slowly! This meat have German hormones."

It was now late July 1991, six weeks since I'd seen Savo in Vienna. We were in Munich, where he lived most of the time. To cool off we'd sat down at a café in the park with lights strung up overhead in the trees. Peg was with us, and Anna, Savo's wife, and their tiny lapdog, Hercules. Savo had arranged for Ahmet and Mehmet, the shadowy Turkish Cypriots, to come to Munich, but so far they hadn't shown up. Peg had arrived a few days earlier, and she was anxiously waiting for Ahmet, waiting for his "proofs." Dikmen himself had vanished; he'd told Savo he was going to Istanbul for a kidney-stone operation. I was hanging around to see what developed, and running up a bill.

I had settled into a rather high-class hotel in Schwabing, not far from the center of the city. A fresh heat wave had swept the streets of virtually all pedestrians except the museum- and church-inspecting sort, and it had also given Munich a Mediterranean glitter, a sharpness of definition, that flattered its neoclassical palaces and would have pleased the nineteenth-century sentimental Bavarian taste for the antique. Occasionally a crowd of young visitors, nearly as naked as Spartan gymnasts, would make a beeline from one scrap of shadow to another. I had tried to keep out of the streets myself, but toward evening, as a tide of cool shadow washed across the city and inched up its spires and domes, I had gone for a stroll on the Leopoldstrasse, and there I spied Peg and Savo and Anna, who had come out looking for me. They were joking and laughing, not at all like strangers whom fate had thrown together, but like old friends.

Now it was night, we were eating, and the ribs we had ordered were a foot long and the beer glasses a foot tall—surreal enlargements that seemed scaled to the stature of Peg and Savo. Hundreds of Münchners had sought refuge here from the ferocious heat; they might have been vacationing in Split or Dubrovnik were it not for the fighting in Dalmatia. Savo sat with a foot up on his bench, one knee raised, and on that knee, Anna, her fair hair swirled up in a chignon, rested her arm and, sometimes, her cheek. With heavy-lidded hazel eyes, she followed the sheepdog and the children, who were threatening to upset the food trays and beer glasses on the table next to ours.

Anna wasn't interested in the mosaics business, which was what Peg and Savo talked about, and she didn't speak any English, but she seemed to understand everything, and if anyone said anything particularly clever, her gaze sharpened.

Halfway through supper, I dropped into the conversation a name that had long troubled me. "Tell me, Savo, who was Dujan?"

"Dujan? Dujan?" He paused. Then he said, "Ah, Dujo! They killed Dujo a few months ago."

"But who was he?"

"He was one Montenegrin pistolero. They look for him in Amsterdam. I think they call him from street phone and then he come downstairs and—" Savo sighted through an imaginary sharpshooter's rifle.

"Who's they?" I asked.

"Colombian marksmen. The same Colombian drug men who will take care of Michel."

"And how do you know this?"

"Some people in my connection," he said. "Listen, I tell you something. Dujo was put in Michel's old hotel, ParkHotel in The Hague. Michel call down to reception, and as soon as he hear that one man with Yugoslav name has checked into hotel, he is terrified, must stay in his room and never go out." Creases of helpless merriment appeared on Savo's face. "Must avoid hotel hallways, avoid windows! Build bunker in room, for two weeks sleeping in bunker!" He said it the German way—*boonker*. With his hands, he showed me how Michel's fortification was positioned relative to the window. "Ha, ha, boonker!" he roared. Then his smile sagged, and the mirth drained from his face. "You know Michel," he said. "What does he say about me?"

I had been hoping he wouldn't get onto this topic—hoping I wouldn't have to tell him Michel's bizarre anecdote about the sting operation on the train from Munich to Amsterdam. Actually, I had tried to forget the story altogether, because I didn't want to get caught between the two of them. Now I saw that I would have to say something. "He told a story about a painting—a painting that was lifted from a train," I murmured.

Savo nodded, and swung into his own version of the tale. Much to my surprise, he found it hilarious; even more to my surprise, his story tallied with van Rijn's except for a few minor details. "I myself wasn't there—it was my friends on that train—but *one hour* after Michel steal this painting I take plane from Munich to Amsterdam, go directly to his hotel in The Hague. I say, 'Give me back painting.' And he give it. Is at home on my wall right now." Then Savo said, "Listen, I'm not angry with Michel now—our fight is over. But you should know that Michel is one man who think only of deception. Every day must think up some new deception before lunch."

One reason I had come to Munich was to talk to the local authorities, which I did the following morning. On this circuit I discovered, among other things, that the Bavarian customs intelligence service, perhaps in conjunction with police and tax inspectors, had raided one of Dikmen's apartments, on the Goethestrasse, about a year earlier. No sooner had this raid been scheduled, however, when word of it leaked to a certain elderly black marketeer and forger (icons, Fabergé) known to insiders as the Old Man, and the Old Man had forthwith tipped off Dikmen. Consequently, the raid, which, according to one underground report, had involved about thirty officers, had turned up nothing whatever—an empty flat. Despite this setback, the customs people had garnered enough information to compile a dossier on Dikmen, a Dikmen File, which had been duly forwarded to the Chief Prosecutor for the region of Munich-I. Questioning customs officers, I asked how much help they had received from Cypriot customs, and they told me that they had received no help from Cyprus at all. Even in the years since Dikmen's name had been publicized at the Indianapolis trial in 1989, the Cypriots had requested no action on the part of the Bavarian authorities. Dikmen seemed to enjoy a strange de facto immunity.

Naturally, I rang the Chief Prosecutor's office and asked if I might come in to discuss the Dikmen File. An assistant prosecutor promised to look it up for me and told me to call back. A day later I did so; he told me there was no one of this name in their records. I pointed out that failure to have any intelligence about Aydin Dikmen would not exactly win them publicity points, and that if they did have the file, they should at least disgorge to me the fact of its existence. The prosecutor firmly replied that it was not their habit to lie to the press: to refuse comment, yes; to lie, no. There just was no Dikmen File.

That same day over the phone, Savo said I should leave Schwabing: he had a good cheap hotel for me on the other side of town. Accordingly, he came around to pick me up in his car, a Spanish Fiat, and we drove west through the city toward Rothkreuz-platz. Peg sat next to him, and I sat in the back, wondering how a putative gangster could possibly be driving this modest, phoneless, middle-class car. He talked to me over his shoulder about Özgen Acar, the Turkish journalist who had long been studying Aydin Dikmen's operations. "After Acar wrote articles in *Cumhuriyet* and *Milliyet* last year, Aydin is put in jail in Konya by Turkish police," he said. "Every police—municipal, military, customs—he is going to Aydin to take money from him. Aydin's brother is driving to help him, driving in Anatolia mountains, when some-body push him off road and kill him. I go to Turkey, deposit documents with Turkish police, and get Aydin out."

"Did you pay money, too?"

"No money. But when Aydin come back to Munich he embrace me. At first he say, 'Thank you, Savo, thank you.' Then, three days later, he start to change. He say, 'You, Savo, bad man.'" Savo looked unhappy about this strange, fickle behavior; his cheeks quivered with disgust.

We swerved to follow the Nymphenburg Canal, which in the heat gave off a stewed-vegetable odor. Savo squinted into the glare of the road. "I think now Aydin wery greedy man, shit-man." He caught my eye in the rearview mirror. *"Il aime trop l'argent. Il est malade,"* he said.

We slowed to pass a row of cyclists slogging along in a strip of shade. "You know, I have some beautiful things, old things," Savo said. "I sell sometimes to Aydin, Aydin pay part, he come back later, try to pay less than he owe me. With some story—I don't know—like rate of exchange; 'Deutsche mark higher, dollar lower.' Over and over, he try to get some nice thing from me. 'Please, please, please, Savo, please,' until finally I must get free from this whining little man. I say, 'Take this and go!' " Savo was practically snorting his words. "You know what I think?" he said. "I think Aydin *must* lie. If he tell me, 'Now I go out and walk on right side of street,' then he must walk on left side. This man does not know how *not* to lie."

Schloss Nymphenburg appeared at the end of the canal, miragelike, trembling in a purplish haze of heat. We pulled up beside a sunbaked inn, which seemed to doze behind lattices closed to keep out the glare. At the reception desk Savo exchanged a few words with the proprietress, whom he evidently knew, and then Savo and Peg and I mounted the stairs to a darkened, stale-smelling room in back, a sort of container for last week's weather.

Savo said, "I open the shutter. No, I don't." He scotched the white blaze he had just let in. "Well, anyway, here you have all that you had in Schwabing, but at one-third the price."

Bed, table, armoire, bath, ten-stroke oil of San Giorgio Maggiore—he was right. I heaved my duffel onto a chair. "Savo," I said, "where are Ahmet and Mehmet?"

"I try to call Ahmet in one hour," Savo said.

I looked at Peg.

"I roared at Ahmet over the phone," she said. "I threatened bodily harm." She threw me a glance conveying all the bitter irony of her position.

"First they were coming in a week," I said. "Then

they were coming in a few days. Then they were coming the next day. Now Savo's calling them in an hour. Ahmet and Mehmet, Mehmet and Ahmet."

"They are still in Cyprus," Savo said, shaking his head.

"What is Mehmet's last name, anyway?" I persisted. "Mehmet what?"

Savo gave me a severe look. "Name? Name? Is Turkish *barbar*. Does not need name."

I decided to drop it. "What's his job?" I asked.

"No job," Savo said. "Is wery hot here." He flopped down on the bed, his huge frame sprawled across its rust-colored synthetic coverlet. He hugged his stomach. "I begin to get fat now—over one hundred kilos. Is too hot for one man getting fat."

"Please tell me about Mehmet," I said.

"Mehmet used to work as museum director," Savo said. "Director of military museum—Ottoman uniforms or something."

"Ottoman uniforms?"

"Listen, I myself am wery annoyed at this man," he said. "Want money for everything, for every help— this is fucking Turkish mentality! I have spent thousands and thousands of dollars of my money on mosaics—on proofs so I can sell mosaics. Ahmet have proofs, Mehmet have no proofs. Ahmet want to come to Munich or Istanbul to give the proofs. Mehmet want only to go to Istanbul, to spend money on drink and play with *fatimas*. Ahmet is one wery good man. Mehmet is one wery bad man."

"So forget about Mehmet."

"But Mehmet have some grip over Ahmet."

"Oh."

"I will put check for Ahmet and Mehmet in escrow

with Aydin's wife, Koca, some hours before bank close on Friday. This attract Ahmet and Mehmet. Also make Aydin start to think and worry."

Now I was getting confused, but I figured that, just as Mehmet had some grip on Ahmet, Ahmet had some grip on Aydin. Maybe it was a kind of daisy chain, in which some of the players had "the goods" on others.

"What's Koca like?" I asked. "Is she a dependable person?"

"Yes, I think so," said Savo. "She is Orthodox, she go to the church. But she is one gypsy woman, make spells, put curses. Even Aydin is afraid of her. *Elle a beaucoup de phobies.* She is wery afraid of the Devil—maybe because of cutting off that piece."

What piece did he mean, I wondered. Was he imparting a secret again? As so often before, I felt baffled, behindhand, like a latecomer to a play, a man searching for his seat in the darkness while he tries to figure out an incomprehensible plot. Savo let his eyelids droop and seemed to slumber in the semidarkness of the shuttered room. Outdoors it was quiet, except for the occasional sound of a child splashing in the courtyard below.

"Savo," I said, "are you telling me that this dependable, churchgoing Orthodox woman cut the Hand of Mary and the Feet of Christ off a rare old icon?"

"She persuade Aydin to do it," Savo said, yawning. His voice seemed to come from far away now, to speak of doings in the distant past, doings that no longer mattered. "He don't want to, but I think she persuade him. She wery sad to sell whole icon, so beautiful, so sacred, and worth big money. So she persuade him to cut off the Feet. He don't want to, but she make him."

Savo rubbed his eyes and sat up. He forced himself off the bed. There was that check to attend to.

To understand Savo, you had to know about the Drobnjaci clan. He told me this as he filled up his Fiat with smoke. He'd parked on the Luisenstrasse and rolled up the windows and lit a cigarette. It was the evening after my move out to the inn by Schloss Nymphenburg. We were alone and both feeling at loose ends, because by now it seemed very unlikely that Ahmet and Mehmet would ever show up.

The Drobnjaci clan pretty much ran the show in the Drobnjaci Mountains, Savo said; they always had. Like the Serbs as a whole, who for centuries were governed by princes who were also prelates, the Drobnjaci people were led by a sort of chieftain-priest, and Savo's ancestors had occupied this post for thirteen generations. His grandfather had been the last Kujundzic to do so; he had emigrated to Chicago, but when the time came to fight the Austrians and the Albanians, in 1914, he returned to Montenegro and assumed command of a military unit. He didn't wish to be a fighter, but he fought fiercely when his homeland was threatened. "He killed too much," Savo said sadly.

The Kujundzic family traced its origins as far back as the fourteenth century, but now very few people of that name were left in Montenegro, because every time the Serbs fought the Turks, more Kujundzic men died. Savo expressed dismay over recent political developments in Belgrade, yet it was clear that he nursed deep patriotic sentiments. He spoke reverently of Stephen Dušan, the fourteenth-century Serbian em-

peror who successfully held the Turks at bay and conquered much of the Balkan territory once held by
Alexander the Great: it was the Serbs, he said, who in
those days had borne aloft the banner of Christian
civilization.

"In this time Europeans still *barbar*," Savo told me,
grimacing like a medieval European savage and drumming with his hands. "Europeans still eating with fingers, but Dušan insist on knife and *Gabel*."

"Fork?"

"Yes. Then he is given poison and he die. Turkey is
coming back, win Battle of Kosovo in 1389, but Montenegro don't accept Turkey, never accept Turkey."

Savo's father had been a naval officer, stationed in
Split. Like most Montenegrins, he felt a deep kinship
with the Russians, traditional protectors of the South
Slav peoples. In 1948, at the time of the rift between
Tito and Stalin, Tito had imprisoned 6,000 Montenegrin military men because he was unsure of their political orientation, and one of them was Savo's father.
He spent three years in prison, where he contracted a
pulmonary illness of which he later died. "He was
big, strong," Savo told me. "Compared to my father
I am small man."

I could see why Savo appealed to Peg. In the Middle
West, where he'd given his sworn statement, his powerful physique and foreign appearance had aroused
some suspicion, but his appearance put Peg in mind of
her father, the Jewish plant manager, who was also
tall and dark and had always adored her. To those
disposed to like him, Savo's curiously martial quality,
which wasn't stiffness but a sort of war-college chum-
miness, suggested a positive gift for comradeship, and
characteristically he had taken time to listen to Peg,

whom he called "the lady," and had seemed to accept her side of the story. He respected her, and as far as I could see, they were close friends now.

Yet there was something about Savo's power to call forth trust that offered cause for puzzlement. No human relations are possible without trust, and in the end, as Peg had obviously concluded, one has to have faith in *someone*; but in a way trust also means weakness, lowered defenses, and even, sometimes, unconditional surrender. In conversation Savo casually revealed an impressive familiarity with such subjects as artillery, wiretapping, private investigation, and document authentication ("Typewriter does not make exactly same marks on two different days," he told me once, to my astonishment), and doubtless all this sounded exhilarating to Peg, who felt in need of such expertise; yet he was also given to airing statements that painfully stretched one's credulity. For instance, he told me over and over that the dome of the Lysi church had fallen unbroken to the ground, necessitating a "rescue" operation for the frescoes inside; in fact, no dome could survive such a fall, and in any case, recent photographs existed of the intact structure. To accept such notions one had to abandon all one's natural skepticism; had Savo himself really done so, then, and did he expect me to do so, too? There was a certain stylistic anomaly in his behavior: his innate southern friendliness seemed to encourage a teasing, doubting response to his claims, but any actual teasing met with dismissive, beetle-browed inflexibility.

*　　*　　*

A few hours after our conversation on the Luisenstrasse, Savo and I, together with Anna, Peg, and the lapdog Hercules, went into a hotel lounge on the Schützenstrasse, a few doors down from the building where Dikmen lived and perhaps hid many of his treasures. It was a postmodern lounge in pinks and creams, with indirect lighting in the moldings, a bar beneath a coved illusionistic ceiling—trompe l'oeil treetops and clouds—and a barman shaking a shaker and a bald lone middle-aged barfly. We sat down in an alcove, and Hercules scampered off under Anna's watchful eye.

Soon Peg and Savo were deep in a discussion of Peg's fateful purchase of the Kanakariá mosaics in Geneva, in July 1988. Of course, I knew the story from Peg's point of view—I recalled in vivid detail how she had settled in at the Hôtel des Bergues, how she had been shown the mosaics at the airport by an elderly, ailing man, and how she had given Ronald Faulk that huge heap of cash in exchange for the claim tickets to the pieces—but I had no idea how the transaction had appeared from Aydin Dikmen's perspective. Now, however, I gathered that Dikmen had related much of the episode to Savo. Savo hadn't been in Geneva himself, but as he felt his way forward through the story, reconstructing, with Peg's help, the events leading up to the moment when the money had changed hands, he began to convey the eerie sensation that he had somehow witnessed the entire transaction. It was as if just by imagining it all keenly enough, he could insert himself into the past, take spectral form in the air outside the Hotel InterContinental, pass through the lobby with its elegant shops, go up the escalator, float down the long corridors, and noiselessly enter the room, all beige and quilted, where the flesh-and-blood Aydin Dikmen, nervously consulting his watch, was packing his bags to check out of the hotel and flee from this wretched deal. Because that, Savo said, was surely how it had been: Dikmen had gone to Geneva, waited two days, felt the mounting pressure of his affairs in Turkey, and all that time his money had never arrived. On the last afternoon, he had waited and waited in his bank—it was right across the street from the bank where Peg had gone to wait for her money to be transferred from Indianapolis—hoping to deposit the proceeds of the sale. And then his bank's closing time came, so he had to stand outside, while Ronald Faulk tried to reassure him; and Dikmen told Faulk that he must have his money by nightfall or the deal was off. Looking inward, Savo kept on remembering what he had never seen: Faulk imploring Aydin to hold on for just a few more minutes, Faulk running back and forth between the two banks, then Aydin going back to his hotel, the money finally coming through from Indianapolis, and the sum being counted out in hundred-dollar bills—a little over a million dollars. And Peg and Faulk stacking it in two gym bags—how heavy it was!—and Faulk rushing Dikmen's share to the lobby of the InterContinental, where Dikmen stood ready with his luggage, and the two of them going back upstairs to count the money again and sign the bill of sale, and Aydin not even keeping a copy for himself as he fled from his room and down the escalator and past the shops in the lobby and out into the thickening dusk.

When Savo had finished, Peg said, "You know, I

have the feeling that I saw the real Aydin back then. I saw him as a blur across the street—I didn't have my contacts on—but I was afraid of going over to him, afraid of spooking him. I realize now that he must have been standing outside his bank, waiting for the money. The funny thing is that I could swear I saw somebody else standing beside him—an absolutely enormous man."

Savo nodded. "Sunglasses?"

"Yes."

"Wolfgang," Savo said. "Tiny Gianfranco Ferrè sunglasses, wery comical on 200-kilo German man."

"I could have walked right over to them," Peg said. "Later, Aydin told me that he would never have sold me the mosaics if he had known who I was." She fetched one of her huge sighs. "I suppose it's because I'm a woman," she said.

"Yes."

"He would have been afraid that I'd dispose of the mosaics too publicly, and at too high a price," she said.

"Yes."

"And if I'd talked to him he would also have discovered the huge difference between what I was paying and what he was getting."

"Yes." Another voice was speaking—higher and hoarser than Savo's. "At last you have figured it out," said the voice. "Bravo! Bravissimo!"

We looked up. The voice seemed to have come out of nowhere, but there by the bar, holding his beer glass aloft and looking down at us, was the barfly we had passed on entering. He was a pudgy fellow with soft features, like dumplings, and a pair of thick glasses behind which glistened two little eyes full of malice and mock deference. He bowed from the waist toward Peg, like an old-time Prussian officer, and took a foaming sip of his beer. On his chubby, dainty hand flashed a gold ring set with a huge amethyst.

"Who are you?" Savo said, disconcerted—it was the first time I saw him so.

"Just a tourist," said the man, with an insinuating smile. "Just a very special sort of tourist." His English was fluent to the point of slipperiness, and German-accented. To my astonishment, Savo merely turned away from him, like one not caring to acknowledge a phantom, and went on talking to us, in somewhat lower tones. He seemed to be denying the man's presence, and I saw that this denial, in the demimonde of antiquities trading, was tantamount to a kind of virtuosity: Savo felt he could throw away secrets as a pianist tosses off bars of sixteenth notes. He said to Peg, "The only reason that Aydin sell you the mosaics is that he don't know who you are."

"He knew exactly who she was," the man with the amethyst ring broke in; and suddenly I felt really alarmed. His objection seemed plausible, even rather shrewd, and if he, too, was a player in this intrigue, then Peg and Savo had just betrayed themselves to an agent whose identity was wholly unknown. Yet Peg, like Savo, ignored him.

"When I met Aydin in Munich," she said, "he told me that he had thought the mosaics were going back to Leventis—to Cyprus."

"How convenient," said the amethyst man, but we all continued to snub him.

Then Peg said to Savo, "You know, right before the trial I got hold of the picture of Aydin that had appeared in *The Independent*, and I said to Joe Emerson, 'Joe, that's not the man I met at the airport in Geneva.'"

"I have seen photo of the man who shook your hand there," Savo said. "Wery good choice, really. He look like Aydin—at least 60 percent Aydin. Have dark glasses, like Sicilian Mafia—like this American actor on TV, he play role of lawyer—"

"Raymond Burr," said the amethyst man.

Savo glanced up at him. "Yes, like this Raymond," he said grudgingly. "Michel had photo of him. When I was in Amsterdam, Michel take me into his boonker, show me one piece of Samsonite luggage with all documents on mosaics, including one photo of this false Aydin, a friend of Michel's who owns restaurant in Geneva."

"Why would Michel want to show you that?" I asked.

"For a while, when there was peace between us, Michel show me many things," Savo said.

"Aha!" said the amethyst man.

Savo looked up at him and said sternly, "You are not at my table. You are not my guest."

"But I am a guest of the hotel," he replied, with a cheeky smile.

All this time, Anna had been watching her dog as he poked about the bar. But now the amethyst man had engaged her attention with his rudeness, and all at once she stood up and fixed him with her big hazel eyes. *"Sie sind zwar Gast des Hotels, aber Sie sind nicht unser Gast!"* she said fiercely.

Reprimanded by a pretty woman, the man looked crestfallen, discountenanced. He turned away, exchanged a few phrases with the bartender, then suddenly turned back and stared straight at Savo. "I know you," he said scornfully.

Savo's jaw dropped, and his face took on a worried expression. "You do not know me," he said.

"But I do," said the amethyst man. "And I know your country very well."

"What country?" Savo asked.

"Montenegro."

"And what is your country?" asked Savo.

"My country? It is not a country. *Ich bin ein Berliner*"—he bowed again, and looked at Peg and me with his insinuating smile—"as your dear departed President once said."

"Do you know my name?" Savo said slowly.

"Your name is not important," said the amethyst man.

Savo looked around at us with evident relief. "He knows nothing," he said. "Ignore him."

Savo returned to his story: he began to draw a diagram of Michel's room at the ParkHotel on a paper napkin. He put in a table and chairs and the famous boonker, and then he put in the picture window that looked out over the park behind Queen Beatrix's palace.

"Michel told me he moved into that suite so nobody could shoot at him," I said.

"But somebody *could* shoot at him," Savo said coolly. "From here." He drew an arrow just outside the window—out of range, I supposed, of the electronic sensors in the park.

I thought about this for a few moments. Then I said, "Tell me, Savo, how did you know Dujo?"

"Dujo was one Montenegrin bang-bang man everybody know," Savo said. "I know him from child-time. He is criminal, yes, but wery sweet, like baby. He kill only bad men, never for money. And after two weeks Aydin take Dujo away from Michel's hotel. Aydin feel sad for Michel. He know Michel too well, too long. So he take Dujo away."

"Why was Dujo put there in the first place?" I asked.

"Why do you think?" Savo said, and gave me his severe look. "Michel cannot be arrested, has corrupted Dutch police. One day he ring me up, speak French, then suddenly change to English. Why change to English? So police, who are taping our conversation, will understand! His tricks are so obvious. Michel is medium, medium-low in the head. He sell good pieces, but is not intelligent, not cultivated. One thing, though: he have wery good nose for donkeys. Oh, excellent nose for donkeys!"

Peg didn't even smile; she just sat there quietly, toying with her drink.

"Michel has no self-confidence," Savo went on. "Doesn't know where he come from, who he is. Only know how to lie."

"He thought you were a fool for telling him where and when that painting was coming across the border," I said.

"I told him the *truth*!" Savo said angrily.

"Well, I didn't," I said. "I was kind of put off by all the stories about bodyguards and gunmen, so I told him I'd arrive in The Hague on one train and deliberately took another. I thought I was being cautious, but actually I almost blew it. In one of my conversations with Michel, I unthinkingly mentioned Marko, Draža, and Hans by name, and he immediately figured out that I knew who they were—he is quick, Michel, very quick. So I made up a fib about having learned their names at the Indianapolis trial, and I guess that got me off the hook. I've never in my life had to think so fast." Briefly I felt a dark maverick pride that I had played this game with Michel—that I'd contended with him for a moment—and I flew so high on the wings of my anecdote that I failed to notice the scowl forming on Savo's face.

When I'd finished speaking he said to me softly, almost despairingly, "Now I know that you lie."

Peg looked away, and Anna masked her eyes with a hand. I tried to look unconcerned, but Savo's gaze trapped my features in what I sensed to be an artificial smile. During months of wandering through a world of masquerade, I had never wondered whether I myself could be swallowed up by the maze. Yet I had ventured forth on sufferance, I had penetrated this world like a boy in a fairy tale with a prohibition ringing in his ears; and now I had broken that prohibition, and had to try, however feebly, to dodge the consequences.

"I can't believe," I murmured, in a voice that sounded foreign to me, "that you, Savo, wouldn't have acted precisely as I did. I'd never met Michel, I'd only heard stories."

"Is nonsense," said Savo. "Listen to me now. I never lie, because I don't have to. I have self-confidence. I know who I am, who my people are. I am not the son of some *putain*! If things do not go well for me one day, I don't need to lie, because they will go well for me some other day. I tell you, I *never* lie."

Savo was almost bellowing now, and I realized that I'd forgotten about the eavesdropper, the amethyst man. I looked up anxiously to see what he made of all this. But there was nobody left at the bar—nobody but the bartender, reading a magazine. The hotel lounge was deserted, except for Anna's little dog pirouetting on the rose-colored carpet.

We left the lounge and got back into Savo's Fiat, where I sat silently, worrying about the amethyst man and all he had heard. The thought crossed my mind that he could be a favored client of Dikmen's—maybe a merchant staying at a hotel convenient to the Turk's flat. Or he could be a customs agent, or a policeman assigned to Dikmen's case. Or, for that matter, a buddy of Dikmen's. Or an enemy. Or a nobody—a tipsy intruder with the gift of repartee.

After my blunder in the hotel, Savo clearly had an altered view of me. But what I got from his view of me was limited: a trace of regret confined to this mission, a sense that I'd entered a game and lost. It was bad luck, really—a mischance: the evil eye had caught up with me and caused me to act out of character. Only because I was so unpracticed at lying, I told myself, had I made the bad liar's typical mistake of getting carried away by his lie; the possibility that I was unpracticed only because of poor aptitude, or for that matter a mere absence of opportunity, I chose not to consider. As for my own feelings toward Savo, they were different, I realized, from what I'd thought them to be. I had thought of him as an informant, but there was some part of genuine fellowship in my enjoyment of him. There was an appreciation of his gallantry toward Peg, and a growing awareness that he was most informative, simply, about his own emotions: about his attachments and animosities, his feelings of displacement, his unease in a society hostile to

Slavs. About Savo I knew almost nothing substantial, but I knew a few things about myself, and one of them, I was now forced to admit, was that I'd taken a keener pleasure in life since I'd begun my investigation of the mosaics case. I was a person without a fixed address or steady job, a sort of nomadic *Luft-mensch* who happened to love beautiful things, and being in contact with people like Savo had come as a kind of release to me, a weird kind of validation.

As Savo drove me out toward Nymphenburg, I pondered all these perplexities. Gradually, my thoughts began to wander, and two entirely different problems loomed large in my mind. One was the erosion of Savo's presumed faith in Dikmen's word, which, it seemed to me, discredited those of his own revelations which were plainly derived from the Turk. At one time or another, Dikmen had told Peg, Savo, and, apparently, Ahmet that he had never knowingly sold Peg anything, that he had thought he was returning the Kanakariá mosaics to Cyprus, that the sale was a fraud, and that he himself, as seller, had been impersonated by an agent of Michel's. But if Savo no longer gave credence to Dikmen's word—he who had been Dikmen's friend and associate—why should anyone else give it credence? By all accounts, Dikmen was a morbidly evasive man, and surely he had his own motives for asserting that the sale was fraudulent.

The other troubling thing was my failure to examine how the mosaics had been reclaimed from storage at the Geneva airport in order for Peg to inspect them. At the trial, nobody had paid much attention to this, because the notion of a pseudo-Dikmen hadn't really come up. Now, however, after hearing Peg's conversation with Savo, something dawned on me: If Dikmen had been paid for the mosaics only just before leaving Geneva, then when Peg had been accorded a glimpse of the pieces at the Geneva airport, he had still had possession of them. Yet since he himself hadn't shown them to her—another person had—he had to have entrusted the claim checks to that other person. And this made sense only if the other person was Dikmen's agent—or as much Dikmen's agent as anyone else's. Dikmen may even have been at the airport all along, to keep an eye on his goods. Peg wouldn't have recognized him; she didn't know him from Adam. He could have been the fellow standing by the wall reading *Die Zeit*, or the fellow standing with his back to her by the baggage-deposit counter.

As Savo pulled up outside my hotel, I put the obvious question to him: "Savo, are you still friends with Aydin?"

"Oh, Aydin!" Savo said. "Before, he call me *Bruder*, kiss my hand, kiss foot. Mmm-wah! Mmm-wah! Now Peg come looking for him, and he hide, put head in sand, like this bird—"

"The ostrich. Listen, Savo, your feelings about Aydin seem to have changed a lot. When I first met you, you told me that he was a good man. You stressed his goodness. Now you have contempt for him. He's a liar, a Turkish *barbar*, and so on."

At this, Savo gave me his most reproving look—a look you might give a persistently inattentive child. "I never said he is good," he said. "I said he is good *for Cyprus*. He help Cyprus by saving things—mosaics, frescoes—from fanatics and vandals. And I never call him Turkish *barbar*! I think he is one shit-man, Aydin, but never *barbar*."

6

I arrived in Cyprus in early September 1991. At almost the same time, the four Kanakariá mosaics that Peg had lost at the trial also arrived and were duly uncrated. I saw them sitting in a back room of the Byzantine Museum in Nicosia—I had never set eyes on them before. During the lawsuit they had been entrusted to a neutral art shipper, then they had gone on display at the Indianapolis Museum, and now, finally, they had come back to Cyprus. As I scrutinized them I saw that they had spiritual power: a person of mystical bent might have maintained that they had traveled halfway around the world and back as part of some providential design. But they also looked faded and terribly forlorn, and I felt that they would always look that way until they could be reinstalled in the church of Kanakariá—until, at last, they could go home.

I had thought about visiting the church of Kanakariá, but not having the heart to contemplate an interior stripped of its splendor, I journeyed west instead, to several remote Byzantine churches whose decorations were intact. Tiny basilicas of rustic masonry, often surmounted by a squat cupola scarcely broader than the wingspan of an eagle, they usually stood high in the mountains, on the edges of hollows or ravines, and near villages that the routes of commerce had long ago abandoned to a dignified impoverishment. Monkishly aloof from the melodramatic geological formations about them, they seemed anchored, like outcroppings of bedrock, against the depredations of man and nature.

From my inn in the Troodos Mountains, only a dirt road, rutted and swirling with dust, led to the ancient church of Panagia tou Arakou, near the village of Lagoudera. For an hour's drive, the road galloped and hairpinned through savagely eroded declivities; vistas of ribbed and pockmarked uplands moved brusquely in and out of sight, and amid the sparse pinewoods and dried-out olive orchards an arid white soil showed, like the raw hide of an afflicted beast. Long, curving terraces looked all but abandoned to the wind and rain, though over them here and there brave attempts at reforestation pushed hard against the sandy wasteland.

It was noontime, and fiercely hot, when I reached the church. Its interior turned out to be entirely covered with frescoes in a scheme of gold ocher, warm white, dull blue, and rose madder. One's impression was of being completely surrounded by a small pictorial Bible—of actually living inside the Bible— because the paintings gave a fairly complete representation of the story of Jesus and the Blessed Virgin. Down from the dome gazed Christ Pantocrator, the Ruler of All Things, and from between the windows of the drum a choir of twelve dancing prophets—a wonderful figurative invention—proclaimed the coming of the Son of Man. Farther down, on the vaulted ceiling and walls of the church, the Gospel itself was embodied in a series of paintings representing scenes from the lives of Mary and Jesus, and several portraits of saints and early prelates completed the decoration. For anyone familiar with Italian trecento and quattrocento churches, with their great fresco programs, it was the usual assembly, and yet uncommonly poignant; what made it so was the sensation of being tightly wound about—almost swaddled—in joyous color and natural, unforced storytelling energy, the diminutive size of the basilica contributing to the success of the visual narration.

To say that these frescoes were great paintings would be absurd, and yet the painted church was absolutely compelling as a sanctuary, an oasis of divine grace. As its name, *toû arakoû*, announces, it was dedicated to the Virgin of the Pea Plant, perhaps because of an apparition in a field planted with peas; if the shrine is difficult of access today, reaching it in the thirteenth century must have required a considerable expenditure of time and energy. Even then the region was probably as parched and deforested as it is now; after hours in the blinding sun, the wayfarer would have thrust his head into this miniature dome, so like a tiny planetarium, and gazed up at a picture of heaven and its inhabitants; slowly, as his eyes adjusted to the darkness inside, the shapes and colors would have cohered into what he, as a believer, recognized as the very source of his salvation. If the experience had and still has a unique religious force, it is a kinesthetic one, intimately connected to landscape and light, and I wondered if it could ever suffer removal to any other place on earth, be it Munich or Houston or even Nicosia. Can spirituality be crated and uncrated?

The reappearance of looted Cypriot artifacts in Western hands is peculiarly painful to the Cypriots; one reason is that it re-enacts in the cultural sphere some of the humiliation of the colonial condition. Yet confusion and a kind of amateurishness were the hallmarks of the Cypriot efforts to recover stolen treasures. Several Cypriot officials admitted to me that they had no tradition of international police or customs cooperation. In meetings with four different agencies involved in the effort to recover those parts of the Kanakariá mosaic cycle that were still missing, I was given four utterly divergent accounts of how matters stood.

My inquiries led me to hotel lobbies, corridors, antechambers, offices piled high with memoranda and spilled dossiers. I couldn't find people, they couldn't find me, we fixed appointments somewhere in a vast night filled with the fragrance of jasmine, radios wailing lovesick balladry, gaudy wedding receptions, murmurous tides of chatter and laughter. People encountered briefly during the day in government offices would turn up coincidentally in socially remote nocturnal contexts, sphinxlike, unsurprised, as if it were my fate to meet them over and over again. ("But Demetrios is my cousin, of course I am here.") With great fanfare I would be taken to be introduced to someone in possession of confidential information, only to meet the bland functionary with whom I'd just had tea, and who now looked different, troubled and troubling, like his own reflection in a mirror.

One evening, in the office of an investigative news-paperman, a civil servant whom I'd seen the day before suddenly appeared out of nowhere, as if guided by remote control. He asked me whom I was going to meet next, and when I told him that I was to see someone whom I shall call X, he said, "Fine, I will drive you there, X is a very good man." The civil servant was indeed an acquaintance of X—this was obvious when we arrived—but neither of us had the directions to X's house, and his phone line was tied up.

"It doesn't matter," the civil servant said, plunging his jeep into the night. "Everybody knows everybody in that quarter, we'll just ask from street to street."

We meandered through an involution of alleys, vacant lots, prefab projects, houses of ungraspable shape, buildings set at meaningless angles to one another, sidewalkless districts that seemed merely collections of haphazard building sites in which all business meddled in all other business. The civil servant sought X's address among the old men in outdoor cafés, in crowded convenience stores, on terraces where women and girls fanned themselves in the heat. As we drove, huge commercial glass-walled buildings slid by, showing row upon row of sample bathrooms filled with aquamarine and lavender tilework, toilets, bidets, shower stalls, bathtubs, all thrown up in a dim theatrical light against the black sky—buyable oases for a people who knew all too much about homelessness, flight, and thirst.

My Cypriot contacts seemed always agitated, on the run; they had just forgotten something or were late somewhere or were heading unprepared into some challenging situation. They were never dull, never obvious, and I wondered if they were at all typical of this intense, edgy, overalert people, in whose capital nothing seemed designed or geometricized, and in which there were no straight boulevards showing a conventional or ceremonial way to get anywhere. Actually Nicosia was a butt end of a capital, with the Green Line cutting right through the Old City, right through one side of the circular Venetian fortification and out the other: it was like having a wall knifing at some weird angle through a house whose occupants have tried to live together and failed, and who now can't see or hear what those on the other side are doing or saying.

The Greek Cypriot conception of evil had to do with infection, intrusion, people breaking into your house—that was the first level of consciousness; at some deeper level, however, there was an uncomfortable admission that evil also comes from inside every human being, from inside every community, and that the Turks, too, must have their own sense of righteousness, their own moral instruments of self-vindication. Though in Nicosia antiquities are a tourist attraction and a selling point—amphoras and kraters compose tedious, pseudo-ethnic motifs on curtains, rugs, lampshades, and place mats—they are also a way of staking an unbeatable claim, of publicizing the fact that Greeks have lived on the island for three and a half millennia. It seemed that almost everybody had, or had once had, a collection ("I sold it"; "I declared it"; "I froze it"), and everybody with any interest in the topic talked obsessively about illicit trading and influence peddling.

The person in Cyprus who knew more than anyone else about the ongoing attempts to recover the missing Kanakariá pieces was Michael Kyprianou, a parliamentary deputy and an attorney on retainer to the Church of Cyprus; he was the man whose taped conversation with Michel van Rijn had so interested Peg after the Indianapolis trial. A voluble fellow with a foxy expression, Kyprianou told me in his Nicosia office that he had hired a Berlin law firm to look into suing Aydin Dikmen or, less plausibly, into getting him prosecuted. (At the mention of Berlin, I pricked up my ears: I recalled that the eavesdropper in the Munich hotel lounge had presented himself as a Berliner, but I knew it would be unwise to mention this encounter to a person I knew so slightly.) He confided that Michel van Rijn had offered to make all sorts of swaps and deals, which the Cypriots had rejected out of hand. "We don't go around buying back our own property from thieves," Kyprianou said, his voice dripping with scorn. "Van Rijn knows very well that all his stolen icons are useless. He will have to wait a hundred years to sell them." It was clear, however, that Kyprianou didn't know who had the missing mosaics.

I discovered that the agreement between the Menil Foundation and the Church of Cyprus governing the eventual return of the Lysi frescoes—an agreement that had been celebrated by the foundation with great blasts of publicity—was generally looked upon with disapproval in Cyprus, where there was tremendous bitterness over the frescoes' sojourn in Houston. A Cypriot civil servant who had negotiated with the foundation told me that "the dynamics of the conversations" had left him with a feeling of "blackmail": if Cyprus didn't cave in to the foundation's self-serving proposal, he felt, the latter would pull out altogether, leaving the frescoes to their fate. He and his colleagues resented the fact that the paintings had been restored in London, in the strictest secrecy, with no Cypriot participation. After all, weren't Nicosia's own restorers experts at salvaging frescoes? And there was something else that rankled: by now, six years of the fifteen-year term of custodianship had passed, yet the foundation, plagued by financial woes, had never put the frescoes on public display, much less built the chapel it had promised.

More than one Cypriot, recalling some long-past journey to a hamlet on a precipice, spoke to me in reverent tones of some favorite little church in the hinterland. Visits to such places could be long-drawn-out affairs: there was the inquiry at the local coffee-house after the *pappás*, the village pope; the discovery of the *pappás* at work in his vineyard or olive orchard; the expectant walk back through terraced hillsides to fetch the keys to the church; the doors of the church swinging open; the kisses placed upon the icons on the way in; and then, at last, the first view of the light streaming down through the drum of the dome upon walls alive with painted archangels, prophets, and saints—dear old friends who had bestowed their blessings on forty generations of Cypriot children.

At one village perched on a high mountain, not far from Nicosia, I stopped impulsively at the outdoor café to ask where the *pappás* could be found. It was Sunday morning, rather late, and I assumed that Mass would be over, but I was informed that it was not: a decrepit café regular led me through the village to the church at a slow but steady pace, as if to suggest that if the Eucharist wouldn't kill him, it wouldn't cure him either.

I was disappointed to see that this church was not old, but it was attractively rustic, with a roof of slate tiles, walls of irregular stone masonry, and an enclosing hand-hewn wooden frame whose massive and elaborate joinery showed at the corners. My guide resigned himself to a dose of religion and crossed himself as we entered. Inside, the exposed beams, pews, and pulpit proclaimed an unschooled workmanship animated by a prettifying piety. The shafts were all fretted or fluted, the finials capped with hammered brass, and the icons of the iconostasis framed in gold: the rococo frames seemed to dance about the images of Jesus and the Blessed Virgin and Saint John Prodrome. To the left of these obligatory presences stood also a Saint Charalambos, who, like them, was without artistic merit but had exceptional personal appeal: tall, gourd-shaped, solemn-eyed, and with a snowy beard flowing down half the length of him, he looked ready to offer you all the wisdom you might need and some besides. There was about a half hour left of the Mass to be said, which the *pappás* and the cantor intoned before the iconostasis and in the shadows of the sanctuary. It was a liturgy I'd heard countless times before, but this congregation was more ancient than any I had ever seen. Out of fifty or so worshippers, perhaps ten were children, while the age of the rest varied from about sixty to ninety and beyond. The women, wearing kerchiefs trimmed with bright embroidery, stood or sat with the children in the back; the men crowded in front, standing or sitting in high-backed pews that ran along the walls. I had no way of knowing whether these pews, which were like homemade versions of cathedral choir stalls, had been assigned to notables or were available to first comers, but scrutinizing the olive tints, hollow cheeks, and casually grand mustachios of their occupants, I could not imagine a better sample of rustic venerability. Softly defined by the light drifting through the church's tiny clerestory, eyes glazed or shut in the barest slumber, each elder was framed by his own stall and sunk in his own reverie. All the while the cantor's voice rose and fell, smoothly negotiating the meandering melodies but never permitting itself an instant of profane charm.

Soon it was time for Communion, and as I snuffed out my candle and stepped outdoors, my retinal image of the scene inside—the *pappás* with his monstrance, the line of communicants, the hoary Charalambos, the old men bestirring themselves— was also extinguished in the glare of the midday sun. One by one, the men came out and sat on a row of benches arranged in a semicircle. The most elderly wore open jerkins and baggy pantaloons, or *vráka,* which they complemented not with leather top boots, as a costume designer might have wished, but with tall rubber galoshes. Bread and wine were handed around, and they all took out their handkerchiefs to receive the *kólliva* (a mixture of barley, raisins, and pomegranate seeds, consumed in memory of a deceased person or to honor a baptism), which was distributed by one fellow in handfuls from a basket. It was congregations such as these, I reflected, in the forgotten hills and valleys of rural Cyprus, who were

from the Greek Cypriot perspective the most immediate victims of the looting of the island. Their cultural heritage had been maimed forever.

While I was in Nicosia, the big independent daily *O
Phileleftheros* published a series of articles, by Makarios Drousiotis, about the huge number of ancient items
that had been exported from Cyprus by permission of
Vassos Karageorghis while he headed the Department
of Antiquities between 1963 and 1989. Karageorghis
had ruled the department with an iron hand, which
may have been just what it needed during that polit-
ically chaotic period, but he had also made many
enemies in the Cypriot cultural establishment, and it
was obvious that Drousiotis's stories were based on
information emanating from angry persons inside the
department. The most serious allegations were that
Karageorghis had granted twelve hundred export licenses to various individuals for a vastly higher number of objects (sixteen hundred items had been
exported to Switzerland under a single license); that
he had not kept pictorial records of what left Cyprus;
that he had failed to protect ancient tombs at Am-
athounta from being bulldozed for hotel sites; that
during the earlier period of the fortified Turkish enclaves (from 1963 to 1974) he had bought antiquities
on behalf of the Cypriot state from illicit Turkish
Cypriot operators; and that he had failed adequately
to publicize thefts or try to retrieve stolen pieces. (On
October 3, 1985, for example, the restorer at the Byzantine Museum in Nicosia had sent Karageorghis a
memo to the effect that he had seen an archangel from
the great fresco cycle at Antifonitis, a monastery in

northern Cyprus, for sale in London; but Karageorghis had done nothing to recover it.) Perhaps the
gravest charge was that Karageorghis had allowed
many foreign diplomats, including one American, to
remove extensive collections from the island.

The Director of Antiquities does indeed have the
sole right to issue export licenses; the office itself, a
holdover from British colonial days, is unregulated by
any modern democratic legislation. Thus, except for
some petty infractions, Karageorghis did not seem to
have broken the law. But many Cypriots were
affronted by what they regarded as his unseemly conduct and abuse of his discretionary powers. Karageorghis and his defenders responded that he had
released only items of low value—broken things, mul-
tiples, and such like. Still, some of the pieces in question had been donated by the recipients to foreign
museums in order to secure tax deductions—a dis-
maying development in itself.

Karageorghis's no-show at the trial in Indianapolis
had never been convincingly explained, and while not
illegal, it undeniably obstructed the attempts of lawyers on both sides to gather evidence. Now I heard
from a well-placed source in Cyprus that he had flatly
refused to be deposed. Did he have something to hide?
According to the Greek Cypriot press, it seemed likely
that his purchases from illicit Turkish dealers between
1963 and 1974 had in fact been quite extensive. It
might be added that Turkish Cypriot authorities had
long claimed that Karageorghis had commissioned
Turkish Cypriots to obtain artifacts by stealth inside
their enclaves; they also noted that following Turkey's invasion in 1974, the Turkish Army had confiscated numerous unregistered Greek collections,

suggesting—to them, at least—some sort of dubious arrangement.

I visited Dr. Karageorghis in his downtown office in Nicosia. He is a small, courtly, white-haired man, with a high voice and a somewhat buttoned-down manner; he had the aura of one who after many decades of public service is at last free to devote himself almost exclusively to his scholarly labors, from which I had no doubt I was distracting him. When I asked him if it was true that he had refused to testify in Indianapolis, he replied, quite amiably, that it was an absolute falsehood: "I informed my government that I was ready to testify on twenty-four hours' notice, but no official requested me to do so." And what about the Turkish Cypriot trader named Ahmet Aziz—the man who had been telephoning Peg? His allegations—for example, that Karageorghis had dealt directly with Aydin Dikmen—had once seemed rather fanciful, but now seemed vaguely plausible. When I asked Karageorghis if he had ever met someone named Ahmet Aziz, his expression relaxed, and he smiled at his recollection of the fellow.

"Ahmet Aziz was an old crook," he said. "He had an antiquities shop in Konak Square—what the Turks call Atatürk Square—and he had connections all over the island. During the period of the enclaves, I had the right to inspect, for our government, the Cathedral of St. Sophia, and nobody followed my movements. I wasn't supposed to visit people like Aziz—technically, it was illegal—but I was desperately concerned to prevent valuable parts of our heritage from leaving the island, and I bought a lot of things from him for our collections. You must understand that we had no other access to sites within the enclaves—not even our police did. We bought mainly ceramics from him, and also, I recall, an early Bronze Age model of a sanctuary. It seems to me that he had somebody working with him—a young man who made very clever forgeries and concocted 'married' pieces. But I don't think Aziz and his people were of a caliber to have relations with the antiquities mafia—they were just petty swindlers."

"How old was Aziz then?" I asked.

"He must have been well over sixty. A short, chubby man—not in good health."

"Have you heard anything more about him?"

"No, I haven't—only a bird, you know, can cross the Green Line—but his health was very bad at the time."

Silently I totted up the years: Aziz would be over eighty now, whereas his voice in Peg's taped phone conversation had suggested a middle-aged man.

"Are you sure he's really that old?" I asked.

"You know," said Karageorghis, "Aziz must be dead. He'd have died by now, I am sure."

Surveying Nicosia from the high terrace of the Saray Hotel, in Lefkoşa—as the Turks style their side of the capital—you look across a plain of tiled rooftops, here and there etched by a winding street or grooved by a broad avenue. This tableland is also studded, savanna-like, with clusters of minarets, such as the pair that rise over the Selimiye Mosque, originally the Cathedral of St. Sophia, built in the Gothic style by the Crusader dynasty of the Lusignans. At once you see that the architecture of Cyprus is always staking some national claim, even when it reminds you only of rulers long departed—Franks or Ottomans or British. At no time, however, can the abrasion of tribe against tribe or temper against temper have been more architecturally evident than it is today, with the low houses of the Turkish quarter abutting the white cliff of Greek Nicosia's modern tower blocks. The Green Line is clearly legible from the air: it is a matter not only of politics and geography but also of the very tempo of life—the daily music of risings and meals and labors and siestas. Compared with the Greek south, the Turkish north feels becalmed and almost indolent, adrift on a warm tide of custom and convention. The south is hectic, plugged in, internationalized, even somewhat de-Hellenized, whereas the north is relaxed, amiably befuddled, and profoundly traditional, with all the charming amenities of Turkish life.

Foreign observers, though confirming the disastrous looting of Greek Church property in the north since 1974, have tended to see it as a fault of omission rather than one of commission, noting that the Turks know nothing of Christian art and cannot afford the regiment of wardens necessary to guard Byzantine sites; such observers also point out that the Greek side has effectively blocked foreign aid for archaeology and historic preservation in northern Cyprus. My own experiences tended to confirm this view. I spoke with about fifteen Turkish Cypriots—government officials, civil servants in the Turkish Cypriot Antiquities Department, opposition spokesmen, and interested private persons—and failed to detect in their discourse any disrespect for Byzantine art or Greek culture generally: they appeared to realize that it was their pressing duty to salvage what remained of the north's Byzantine heritage, and they condoned nothing that had happened in previous years. There was no doubt that the thievery had been abetted by a certain element of philistine chauvinism, but nobody—including the new director of the Turkish Cypriot Antiquities Department, the liberal-minded Ali Kanli—believed that the ideological factor was of primary importance. The main factor in the destruction of Byzantine monuments was greed.

After making contact with a number of unofficial sources in Lefkoşa, I realized that I had arrived during a lull in an ongoing conflict between, on the one hand, the smugglers and their allies (some of whom were rather well connected socially) and, on the other, certain state archaeologists and the opposition newspaper *Ortam. Ortam* traded information with Özgen Acar, at *Cumhuriyet;* late in 1989, it had published some thirty unsigned articles about antiquities thievery. (The articles were contributed by a concerned civil servant, whose car was torched for his pains.) With the help of interpreters, I began studying these pieces, which gave a detailed and lurid picture of criminal operations on the island.

Then, while sampling an extensive array of homemade yogurts in my hotel room one afternoon, I received a telephone call from two men who'd been deeply involved in the attempt to halt the looting of Greek Orthodox religious sites. Soon they were at my door, and we began a series of confidential meetings with the aim of pooling our knowledge. I wanted, for my part, to learn the identity of the thieves and how they had exported their booty; from the south I had brought with me a list of missing pieces and a detailed description of the materials used in the dismantling of frescoes and mosaics. This technique requires pulling the pieces from their plaster supports with glue-soaked cloth facings, and tests carried out by Greek Cypriot restorers showed that no more than two formulas (an early, crude formula and a later, improved one) had been used in all the operations. The obvious inference, that one group might well have been responsible for most of the looting of churches in the north, matched the information now offered by the two Turkish Cypriots, who had connected a single man, named Hasan Harman, to many of the thefts on the island. At the time of the major robberies, in the late 1970s and early 1980s, Harman had been in his early forties, a thin, fair-skinned fellow with dark brown hair.

"While we were investigating the Lysi robbery," one of my informants told me, "we found two shepherd boys who had been tending their sheep in the neighborhood of the church when the dismantling took place. They saw two men arrive in a blue Ford van, but the men drove away at once when they saw that they were being watched. Soon they came back, this time more furtively, and apparently thinking that they were now unobserved, they got out a long ladder and a bucket of glue and carried them into the church. Later, the boys got a closer look at one of them, a thin, fair-skinned individual in his early forties, with very white hair. At first this description puzzled us, because we didn't know of any white-haired operators, but then, all at once, we understood. His hair was covered with plaster dust from the walls of the church—he was Hasan Harman. Harman is a clever man and a gifted artisan—he got some sort of degree from Middle East Technical University, in Ankara—and with the help of some other men—Mustafa Avçibaşi, Kemal Köse, and Ahmet Kadir Dinç—he stripped many of the churches on the island."

"And the Kanakariá theft? Whose handiwork was that?"

"Pretty much the same crowd, we think, only they pulled it off a few years earlier and with coarser glue, as you know. Later on, when these people read about the sort of prices that the stolen material was fetching in Europe, they were outraged, because they had been paid very little for their work. They'd been hired by a cunning fellow who was going around posing as some sort of state archaeologist—his name is Aydin Dikmen of Konya. A case against him for the theft of the Lysi frescoes has been opened in Famagusta District. But with our legal code, which is derived from Britain's, we cannot try him if we do not have him, and he seldom comes here anymore."

After this unexpected briefing, I started looking for Ahmet Aziz. I poked my head into some haunts on Arasta Street; I questioned the café smokers near the former caravansary; I pestered the crowd of taxi drivers who stood about waiting for fares by the Kyrenia Gate, in the shadow of the Venetian city wall. The café habitués and the cabmen twiddled their key chains and gazed into space, searching their memories; the shop boys turned to call over their shoulders, relaying my query past rows of magazines or batteries or nutcakes to elderly answerers in dim recesses. The old Turkish quarter was a dawdly place, a place of long conversations and slowly sipped coffees, honey, rose water, buzzing flies, obliging smiles, and gestures of accommodation; but no, nobody had heard of an antiquities dealer with the surname of Aziz—unless it was someone who died a long time ago. All the same, I continued my circuit, and just as my patience was beginning to give out, the name Aziz began to elicit a certain hesitant recognition in the halls of notability and officialdom. In high-ceilinged anterooms and shabby-genteel offices, under the omnipresent brooding stare of Kemal Atatürk, guesses were hazarded and conjectures floated.

"Ahmet Aziz, Ahmet Aziz . . . I think you must mean Ahmet Bullici," said one man, a barrister. "*Bullici* means something like 'poulterer' in our dialect—I suppose he must have sold chickens at one time. He's been dead a long while, but I knew him. It is true that he obtained many curious items from the freelance excavators for his shop, off Atatürk Meydani. I remember that he used to tell me about Karageorghis coming to the shop to buy rare things for the Antiquities Department. If I recall correctly, old Ahmet's son was stabbed to death in the Greek quarter, in a cabaret quarrel over a girl or something, but he also had a stepson, tall, thin, with a beard, who worked with him and helped him out. The shop is still there, across from the Venetian Column, but it has changed hands. I think it's a cambio now."

At a government ministry another man said, "This Ahmet chap cuts a figure here. You know him as Ahmet Aziz, but that is not his real name. It is his stepfather's name, which he assumed when he took over his stepfather's shop, many years ago. Here he is known as Sakalli Ahmet, which means Bearded Ahmet. He was in prison in England in the late 1980s for smuggling, and it wasn't for smuggling antiquities, either. I don't know where he spends his days now, but ask around—you will find him. He is charming, and very popular."

Then I ran into a man so knowledgeable that he just took out a pen and paper and began to sketch the way to Ahmet's shop—a new shop, it turned out, for Ahmet had just changed addresses. "Ahmet is actually the biggest smuggler on our side of the island," the man said, in Turkish—another man interpreted for us. "He once pulled a knife on two inspectors from our Antiquities Department. Now he's asking for a license to deal in antiquities again, even though no such licenses have been issued for over fifteen years. For this he intends to go to the courts, but his petition will never be granted. People also say that he's involved in some sort of legal quarrel with the heirs to a dead merchant's stock—he says half the goods are his. I expect that with that half he would try to start trafficking again. He'd be back to his old mischief." As the man spoke, he completed his map. He had put in the Green Line, the Ledra Palace Hotel barricade, and the stoplights at the crossing of Memduh Asaf Street and Selim II Avenue, and on the avenue itself he had put in a yard-goods shop, a nut shop, and then another shop, which he neatly labeled "Ahmet Kadir Dinç."

So Peg's Ahmet was *that* Ahmet! I stared in amazement. I'd known for months about Ahmet Kadir Dinç—everybody knew about him—but I'd unquestioningly assumed that Peg's Ahmet was somebody else. (Ahmet is a very common name.) The trader who styled himself Ahmet Kadir Dinç—*dinç* means "vigorous" in Turkish—figured prominently in Turkish Cypriot government and press reports about smuggling. I'd seen an old newspaper clipping in which a smirking Ahmet advised tourists on how to spirit their illegally acquired amphorae and fibulae out of northern Cyprus. My local contacts had described him as having an excellent grasp of the history and value of Cypriot antiquities and as being clever at forming alliances with traders and politicians; they had also named him as one of those accused of involvement in the stealing of the Lysi frescoes. A fellow widely regarded as one of Aydin Dikmen's accomplices had told the police that he had seen Dikmen in Ahmet's shop at the time of the burglary, and that some fresco fragments had been hidden there for about a week. But the police could not prove much of anything against Ahmet, and he had vehemently denied all the charges made against him. He was sly, elusive, amusing. When I asked my informant when I could find him in his shop, he said to me, "Always—I will take you there."

It was late morning; my guide drove me through the nearly empty streets of Lefkoşa till we came to the zone by the Green Line. Here, where Selim II Avenue dwindles away into the no-man's-land that is the old Ledra Palace grounds, a charmed precinct of memory appeared, a few acres that still bore the imprint of the British colonial period. Tall palms and cypresses had dominion over the neighborhood, and as we arrived, a dreamy scent of jasmine filled the air, causing my guide to slow down and sniff and fill his lungs. But the next moment, sitting bolt upright, he said, "That is Mehmet!"

A burly, fair-haired man was walking briskly toward us.

"Get down, quick!" said my guide. "He mustn't see you with me."

But murmuring something about the inevitable, I jumped out of the car into the sunlight. My guide sped off.

Now I noticed another man—bearded, tall, strong, loose-jointed—standing in front of a shop with his hands on his hips. He surveyed the street in classic bazaari fashion—ten seconds up one way, ten seconds down the other way, then back up again, back down, and so on. The fellow called Mehmet had vanished, so there was nobody in the street but this man and myself. I walked up to him and held out my hand. "Ahmet," I said.

Strangely, he seemed to be expecting me.

"Oh, it's you," he said. I recognized the faintly London speech, those glottal stops, but he was not at all as I had pictured him; the face didn't match the voice. That voice was so ragged from smoking that I had imagined him an older man—gray-haired, timeworn, chastened—whereas he couldn't have been much over forty. His hair and beard were piano black, his frame erect, elastic.

"Got a few minutes?" I asked.

"No problem," he said, and he motioned me inside.

Ahmet's shop was long and narrow, and crowded with antique copper cauldrons and hand-painted narghiles. He showed me to an office in the back, with a few chairs and a cluttered desk, then vanished into a narrow galley behind it and returned in a moment with a cup of Turkish coffee and a glass of water, which he set down before me.

"You are welcome," he said. "I am always here,

come by whenever you like." His smile was very pleasant.

I said, "So, Ahmet, I understand you aim to get your license back."

"Yes, and my solicitor has told me I shall get it," he replied.

"What does the Turkish Cypriot Antiquities Department have to say to that?"

His lips curved into a smile of derision. "You have met Ali Kanli, the department's new director?" he asked.

I said that I had.

"And what is your opinion of him?"

"What's yours?"

He lit a cigarette and dragged on it. Veils of smoke floated out of his mouth. "Look," he said, his voice growing even more gravelly. "Think of a baby. How does this baby first move? He crawls, yes? What does this baby do next? He walks, but in a very shaky way—one foot forward, then the next, side to side. Well, Ali Kanli is like this baby. He has learned to crawl, but he cannot walk properly. Believe me, he knows nothing. He is so scared of the Greeks and their propaganda that he doesn't dare move. To attack Karageorghis, he would need to know what I know. But he knows nothing, whereas I know everything, and believe me, that is a problem for him, because I also know everything about his department."

No one could have denied that Ahmet was handsome, of a handsomeness somehow Oriental, or Middle Eastern, rather than simply Mediterranean. That swarthy tint, that curving scimitar nose, those dark pupils lolling under the long calligraphic flourishes of the eyebrows—perhaps Ahmet's ancestors had been

Phoenician traders or adventurers hereabouts. He had a way of tilting his head back as he spoke, so that his eyes, foreshortened, became almonds, and his mustache turned into a perfect arch, and his beard expanded and grew blacker, more velvety. As he shifted his head this way and that, it seemed to change shape and size against the wall behind him, and it occurred to me that his sort of face shown against a light background formed the principal problem of the old icon painters, which was to give the modeling of a very dark head against a nimbus of gold. Comb his hair with an eggbeater, throw a camel skin over his shoulder, and Bearded Ahmet would have made a perfect John the Baptist.

"Ahmet," I said, "is it true that you were in a British jail for a while?"

He smiled with half his face—it was a cute, stagy smile that would have carried a message of "loucheness" up to the third loges. Maybe he relished the question, for it was clearly a part of his seductiveness to emerge from a past of which there were many contradictory accounts—collectors' reminiscences, police reports, foreign-intelligence memoranda, brittle yellowed press clippings—so that his life in the end grew protean, multidimensional.

"I was six years in jail," he began, rhetorically poking the air with a Bic lighter. "I was arrested with a family who were smuggling something into England—not antiquities, something else. I was innocent, but I was the one they decided to charge, just because I happened to speak English. Oh, if you think there is such a thing as justice in the courts of Great Britain, believe me, you are sadly mistaken! There was no evidence against me. All day long, the jury failed to reach a verdict, and then the judge called them back in and scolded them and forced them to make a decision, and they deliberated for only an hour more and then decided, ten to two, that I was guilty. From six against six to ten to two, in one hour! That is the British sense of fair play!"

"Did your jail term have anything to do with your earlier activities here?" I asked him.

His eyes flashed, and his lips parted, then closed again. He thought for a moment and said, very cautiously, "I have always suspected that the Greeks leaned on the British prison authorities while I was doing time. But don't get me wrong—how would I know? I was in prison, not at embassy receptions. But I have said certain things, true things, about diplomats and UN people—things that I know outraged them."

Up to then, no one had come into the shop, but now a man entered and saluted Ahmet. He was strongly built, though somewhat overweight, with a schoolboy shock of fairish hair, and he wore buff-colored trousers and a cotton shirt striped in black and purple. He was the man I had seen earlier in the street.

So there they were at last—Mehmet and Ahmet, together. The newcomer pulled up a chair and held out his hand. "Mehmet Rasih Savarona," he said. By now, I was beyond being amazed at Peg's failure to get a person's identity straight: in the antiquities milieu, people learned what they wished to learn. Why should Peg have known that Mehmet was a former antiquities director for the Kyrenia District, or that he was said to have been embarrassed into early retirement after court testimony in Kyrenia that he had been involved in the burglary of the icon storeroom in the city's medieval castle in 1981? The Kyrenia prosecutor had accused him of altering the museum's inventory and substituting worthless icons for valuable pieces. Hundreds of paintings had disappeared, but the testimony against him—that of two museum guards and a police-department handwriting expert—had been inconclusive, and Mehmet had not been convicted.

I introduced myself as a reporter and asked Mehmet what he was doing now. He told me that he was pleasantly pensioned off. This was an option in Turkish Cyprus, he explained, to take an early pension, and he had taken it of his own free will—nobody had hounded him into it. Then he admitted that he was suspicious of journalists: they were ill informed and hungry for sensation, and as for the Cypriot antiquities trade, well, they had quite misunderstood it. Remembering pressing business elsewhere, he got up and left.

When he had gone, I said, "Ahmet, have you spoken to Peg recently?"

"Poor Mrs. Goldberg," he said—this was obviously the name by which he knew her—"I feel sorry for her and believe me, I want to help her. But to establish trust in this business you must act honestly, and I do not feel she has acted quite honestly in this affair." He gave me a pained smile and fixed me with his eyes as if I were the miscreant in question.

"How is she dishonest?" I asked.

He mused for a few moments. "Perhaps, after all, she *is* honest," he replied, "but somehow they managed to brainwash her. You see, Mrs. Goldberg has never really understood anything. She went wrong at the beginning. This Michel van Rijn, for instance. Believe me, until all this business started I had never once heard his name. But then, when I was watching a BBC program on the trial taking place in your country and saw him being interviewed by a British journalist, I recognized his face, because he was here, in Cyprus, maybe ten years ago. He was in my old shop more than once. Never as Michel van Rijn, mind you—always as, you know, 'Bill from Denmark,' or something. There was a paper that Mrs. Goldberg produced at the trial—a false export license, signed 'Osman Örek,' that Aydin Dikmen supposedly used to get the mosaics out of Turkish Cyprus. Well, Aydin never possessed or gave her such a document. I believe van Rijn said he got it from Aydin before giving it to her, but this is untrue. Who knows who forged that paper! Well, after van Rijn she found Benjamin, and she listens to this Benjamin, who knows nobody, who knows nothing, who has begun to threaten Aydin. But, believe me, this threatening can cut two ways. I do not know who Benjamin's people are, but do you think Aydin is alone? He is not alone. He is very clever, Aydin."

"It's odd that you talk that way about Savo—I mean Benjamin," I said, probing, "because he seems to like you. He brought a favorable opinion of you to Indianapolis after his trip to Cyprus."

Ahmet made his eyes big and spooky and flashed me a sarcastic smile. I was of no use to him except as a sort of gossip conduit or telegraph service—this was something we both understood—and I sensed now that he was about to transmit a message of particular urgency. He leaned forward on his desk, over his pocket calculator and little pads and flip calendar and the cup of Turkish coffee and the glass of water.

"Benjamin has never been in Cyprus," he said quietly. "He never went any farther than Istanbul. A year and a half ago, he told us to meet him there, at the Pera Palas, and he told Mrs. Goldberg that he paid Mehmet's and my expenses, but believe me, he did not. I did. If he took any money from Mrs. Goldberg to visit Cyprus, then he kept it for himself. And, of course, he *had* to speak well of me, and to say that he knows me and he knows Mehmet and Aydin, because in this way he becomes the broker, he makes himself important to her. You see his psychology. But he is not important."

"Maybe he came here afterward, without your being aware of it."

Ahmet looked at me as if I were crazy. All the while he was talking, he toyed and gestured with the things on his desk: pens, pencils, cigarettes, his lighter. They migrated through his fingers, wiggling around, until it seemed that maybe they were alive and his hands inanimate. Now he'd got hold of a tiny screwdriver, of the sort used to replace the batteries in a pocket calculator, and he said, waving it, "How much money has Benjamin taken off Mrs. Goldberg so far—do you know?"

"I know nothing about it," I said.

"No, I think she would not tell anyone," he said. "But, believe me, all the things Benjamin has said to the court in your country—all this about how he has known Aydin for so-and-so many years, and how he has met Leventis with Aydin in London, and so on and so on—all this is only his word. He has no proofs, no documents. He doesn't really know Aydin, he has never been a friend of Aydin."

"Not before? Before the trial?"

"No, never! Benjamin works Mrs. Goldberg against Aydin, just as he works Aydin against Mrs. Goldberg. Don't you see—he's a double agent! I told her so. I told her, 'Mrs. Goldberg, you are making a terrible mistake!' "

I said, "Benjamin says he has an interest or share in the missing Kanakariá mosaics. He says that he bought them with or from some Turkish Cypriots. Is this true?"

Ahmet smiled with half his face again. "I don't know about that," he said. "I cannot talk about who owns the missing pieces. One day in future, the mosaics will probably go back to the Church—don't get me wrong. But it will take a long time. A very long time."

A pair of young Turkish girls entered the shop, and he briefly attended to them. Then he returned to his desk. "Mrs. Goldberg cannot get the mosaics back now—only money," he said. "She can file a lawsuit, if she can prove that she was slandered by somebody or that there was some fraud on the Greek side. But for this she needs me and two others."

He found a pad and drew three dots on it. "You must think of three points to be connected by a triangle," he said. "Alone, none of us has the necessary evidence. Together, we do. But to make this connection"—he arched his eyebrows—"she needs me."

"And what do you expect in return?"

"Well, you see how things are." He waved around at the shop, once again empty of customers. "The

Gulf War has not done us any good here. And my proposal is perfectly fair. She would help me, I would help her. I and Mehmet and Aydin."

"She has no money," I said.

"Tsss! If she paid two hundred and fifty thousand dollars to van Rijn for some paper during the trial—"

"Really? What paper?"

"These are things that we know," he said. He waggled his screwdriver in the air. "Oh, don't get me wrong. I am very sympathetic to her. But I have told her frankly, 'Mrs. Goldberg, this is business. You've got to be reasonable.' "

He put the screwdriver down and reached for a fluted plastic bottle. Jiggled, it gave off a sweet lemon smell. "I believe we are all in business," he said, flourishing the scent bottle. "So what do we all want? We want this!" He plunked the bottle down on the table. "Money! She needs some." He moved the bottle one way. "And I need some." He moved it back. "It is no good any of us pretending."

"But what sort of proof could you offer her? Proof of what?"

"This I cannot reveal," he said, smiling mischievously and shaking the scent bottle in a warning gesture. "But remember, in the period between 1963 and 1974, the time when we Turkish people lived in enclaves, surrounded by our enemies, my stepfather was already too old to run his shop. I ran it. There was terrible poverty and unemployment then, and some of our villagers had raised illicit excavation into an art. A lot of them really knew the pieces. And, believe me, *I* knew the pieces. One day they called me secretly to a tomb. They were digging things up, and a little after

I arrived they dug up this really beautiful big pot. And I said to them, 'Am I a baby? You put that fake there last night.' 'Shhh-shhh,' they said. 'Shhh-shhh.' Well! At that time I personally sold many things to Karageorghis—he bought many things from people in the Turkish quarter. But where are these things now? You will not find them in the Cyprus Museum."

"Okay, where are they, then?"

The cute smile flickered at the corner of Ahmet's mouth. "Go ask Vassos," he said. He lit a cigarette.

"Okay, Ahmet, but how can you prove all this? Do you have documents?"

He screwed up his face. "Ah, now, this is something I tried to explain to Mrs. Goldberg. I said to her, 'Mrs. Goldberg, we are in the smuggling business. Do you think we do bookkeeping, ledgers? Do you think Aydin has invoices and bills of sale?' No invoices! Aydin never puts anything, anything, anything on paper!"

"Well, where does that leave Peg?" I asked. "She might just as well go after Aydin, then."

"Impossible," Ahmet said, grinning. "Nobody can go after Aydin. Nobody can find him. He is constantly moving—Istanbul, Ankara, Konya. Who knows where this man is? He is running from the police, running from this reporter Özgen Acar—from Acar, who says he knows all about him but has never met him, or maybe once, very briefly. Acar chases Aydin all over. Aydin is made very anxious by this chasing by Acar."

"It's fame," I said. "He's a famous man now."

"Yes, but before all this practically nobody knew anything about Aydin. For many, many years. And now everyone has heard of him. In London, New

York—everywhere. And who has done this to him, do you know?" Ahmet curled his lips inward and wafted out a veil of blue smoke. "It's Mrs. Goldberg. Mrs. Goldberg has made Aydin Dikmen a famous man!"

Now from a minaret the muezzin called out, and the chanting voice, running up and down scales, was like a courier dashing all over the quarter with his news. He was telling us that God is great and Muhammad is His Prophet and we should drop our petty business and get down on our knees and pray.

I said, "The Lysi investigation is still open. There could be some interesting testimony against Aydin. There were those two shepherds who saw men with ladders and cloths and buckets of glue—the same glue that was used to pull the mosaics off the walls of the church of Kanakariá."

Ahmet blew smoke and shook his head disdainfully. "Let us say that Aydin did steal the Lysi frescoes," he said. "Let's just say he did do it, to make an argument. Okay, I ask you: where is the evidence? To make a case you have to have evidence. Shepherd boys, ladders! There is no *evidence* against Aydin Dikmen!"

Suddenly I remembered the sound of Ahmet's voice on the telephone to Peg, saying, "He knows that what I tell, it will be against him." I looked up at Ahmet expectantly, but he rummaged about on his desktop with an air of finality. He pushed the pack of cigarettes and the lighter and the scent bottle out of the way. He found a clean white pad and drew a big dot on it. Then, still holding his cigarette, he drew a line out from the dot in a shallow curve that began looping back toward the dot.

He said, "This dot is Cyprus. This is where everything started. Well, then: where is everything going to finish?"

"Cyprus?"

"Believe me, yes. For Mrs. Goldberg also." He blew smoke. "She should have come to me a long time ago."

7

By the time I left Cyprus, in October 1991, I had become uncomfortably aware that all the actors in this far-flung intrigue had by now become aware of my existence. Some doubtless saw me as a nosy parker, others as a useful messenger boy, but whatever they suspected my intentions were, none of them could have found me impressive. Had I ever shaken hands on a seven-figure deal or dodged an assassination attempt? I was a slow-witted, confused American writer wandering around with a suitcase full of documents.

At this point in the development of the antiquities trade, secret information—whether in the form of papers, lists, or tapes of compromising telephone calls—could net more money than many of the disputed pieces might have fetched some decades earlier. By now I'd conducted hundreds of interviews, and scores of sources called me regularly to volunteer information or disinformation; too much contradictory intelligence was being offered for me to assume, ever, that anyone was telling the truth. Well then: who was lying, who was mistaken, and who was retailing—innocently or not so innocently—the lies of somebody else? It was hard, very hard, to guess: as with the sibyls and oracles, those sacred mouths of old, fantastic permutations were possible.

Most of the traffickers ritualistically entombed their more important secrets, which, glazed with a sort of sepulchral sheen, began to resemble the spoils they sold. There were secrets like tear bottles, secrets like memorial tablets, like mummy portraits, like canopic jars daubed with the staring eyes of the departed. There were secrets that were really only oddments prized out of the dead past. Yet the lies guarding all this secrecy had a strange beauty, like the beauty of cypresses watching over a cemetery. There were lies that you wanted to hear because they exculpated some charming person or fit a pet theory, and such tales were always balm for a while, even if you knew at the back of your mind that they were false. To expose a secret or entrap a liar you had not only to solicit but also to offer confidences—this itself was a kind of haggling—for only your own garrulity could call forth that of the liar. Yet you could easily begin to overplay yourself, getting all smarmy and sincere, until you saw that you'd given away a lot and got back nothing in return. Then, too, you were always making a polite show of being convinced, and such play-acting grew duplicitous in itself, so that the liar could begin to see you as one of his own kind, only not very adroit, a failure, and he might despise and deceive you even more. It was disagreeable, and possibly dangerous, to confront a liar with his lies, but if you didn't people would unnerve and humiliate you, saying, "He's lying, don't you see?" And then, into the bargain, you'd discover that *they* were lying.

In this social milieu there were some who didn't lie, but even they, I felt certain by now, were dwelling in the anxious shadow world of the unsaid. And since they had chosen to live in this world, didn't they have to love it somehow, didn't they have to glory in their own compulsive withholding of information, their superiority to the ignorant and uninitiated, their metamorphosis into vessels empty of everything but a few whispering leaves inscribed with prices and phone numbers and guilty names? And since people were so often lying to them, didn't they have to like, to enjoy, being lied to? Didn't they aid and abet the mendacity?

Of course, it is true that by having secrets to trade you gained leverage over people, but your secrets stifled and corroded you; then, because you didn't want to feel or look paranoid, because you didn't want to reveal your universal distrust, you began to let your guard drop, to forget that you, too, were under surveillance. You were, all the same, being watched, you were subject to the evil eye, and the forces casting the evil eye know better than you how to defend their mental property, how to keep from leaking information, from gradually giving in to verbal incontinence. They, after all, were professionals, used to shielding what they knew or suspected, used to maintaining labyrinthine cover-ups. Softly, by degrees, they would break you down, see through your childish dodges, decipher your intimate codes, throw you a thousand bum steers. And you, poor fool, had to keep on smiling, to pretend to be indebted for all that useless information, and the more you pretended, the bolder they got, until they threw you a swift sucker punch.

Though my path had by now diverged from Peg's, we kept in touch by telephone, which, along with its avatar, the fax, was clearly the true medium of the shadow world to which we both provisionally belonged. I had long known that Peg was as fearless as the Atalanta of ancient rhyme; what I was beginning to understand was how greatly the culture of private investigation and legal vendetta appealed to her spirit. At times I felt that I was talking to a seasoned lady detective, and that the whole of Peg's life, all her personal and professional experience, had formed a mere prelude to this, her last and only authentic incarnation. I envisioned a television series called *Goldberg*, with Peg as its granite protagonist. She told me she'd threatened Aydin with a lawsuit, sent him a demand letter for the million she'd lost; she told me Ahmet had had to "scrape poor Aydin off the ceiling." Yet despite her toughness and her instinct for the chase, something in her predicament remained beyond remedy: it was the very dilemma on whose horns Tom Kline had once impaled Joe Emerson. The more sophisticated she seemed, the more she tended to put her informants on guard against her; the more naïve she seemed, the more likely it was that they would try to take her to the cleaners.

As the weather finally cooled off and autumn set in, I found myself lost in a cacophony of claims and counterclaims. By this point I had stopped wandering around—I had settled in Italy, outside Florence—and in November I journeyed to London to meet Constantine Leventis. Leventis, of course, had been the linchpin of the Cypriot case in Indianapolis in May 1989, having testified that the Cypriots knew nothing about

Aydin Dikmen until that very year. Numerous under-
cover traders had laughed at this claim, yet as soon as
I saw him I realized he was not well cast for the part
scripted for him in the rumor mill of the antiquities
world. Where a superbly self-confident secret-agent
type would have been required, here was a short,
slightly rounded man in spectacles, scholarly-looking,
modestly dressed, and quite devoid of the imperious-
ness of the very rich. After we had conversed for a
while, I introduced the subject of Savo Kujundzic's
sworn statement to Peg Goldberg's lawyer, made a
year after the Indianapolis trial. Leventis seemed
merely amused by it. "He said that I was thin and—
what was it?—arrogant," Leventis said, and gave me
a wry look, as if to suggest that he couldn't pull off
arrogance if he wanted to.

I said, "Kujundzic stated that you met Aydin Dikmen about nine years ago, at Sotheby's."

"I've never met Mr. Dikmen in my life. The first
time I heard Mr. Dikmen's name was a couple of
months before the Indianapolis trial. Many years earlier, at the time of the salvaging of the Lysi frescoes, I
asked Yanni Petsopoulos to give me the name of the
man who possessed the frescoes, but I saw that he
wasn't going to do so. Mr. Petsopoulos is a dealer,
and I suppose dealers have some sort of etiquette
about sources. He told me the source's story about the
frescoes' Anatolian provenance—how at first he'd believed it and then changed his mind. But that's only
what he told *me*."

"In your deposition," I said, "you stated that you
have no art collection. Many people say that you do."

"Oh yes, I do have one," he conceded. "I must have

misunderstood the question. But it is true that I have no Cypriot pieces. Other antiquities, yes. Nothing very valuable."

I asked him, "Do you know where the rest of the Kanakariá mosaics are?"

"Not really," he said. "No more than what the Cypriot government tells me."

There was little, I realized, that anyone could do to recover the hundreds of Christian antiquities stolen from Cypriot churches. Most had gone to Munich, where a handful of dealers plied their trade—some less than honestly. From Munich many pieces had proceeded to Amsterdam or London, and a select few had ended up in the hands of auctioneers. Stolen icons cannot usually be flogged on the market unless they have first been cleaned and restored, and here the former restorer Stavros Mihalarias, who is now an auctioneer in Athens—and who, incidentally, claimed to me that he could not recall having acquired the British Museum's Saint Peter from Michel van Rijn—might be able to offer valuable information.

Every once in a while, a Cypriot visiting an icon exhibition in London feels a tug at his heart as he recognizes the style of some familiar Cypriot painter, or recalls a glimmering iconostasis, half veiled by the incense of sorrowful memories, that perhaps bore the holy image now before him on the gallery wall. In November 1991, an icon of Saint John Prodrome was removed from a sale at Sotheby's after protests from the Church of Cyprus. The Church's attorneys produced affidavits from several old men bearing witness to its original place in the iconostasis of a church in a northern Cypriot village. They soon learned that the icon had been consigned to Sotheby's by none other than the Menil Foundation's former agent Yanni Petsopoulos, and at a hearing before the High Court of Justice in London, in April 1992, he acknowledged that he had indeed done so, and would refuse to hand it over unless compelled. The court ordered the piece to be delivered into the custody of a respected art shipper until rightful possession should be decided.

After the hearing in London, I called up Petsopoulos, who defended his behavior eloquently on the phone. "I told the Church's lawyers that they had no case—that I wasn't the owner, and his name didn't concern them. I have good reason to believe that the piece is not stolen."

And what about his involvement in the sale of the Lysi frescoes?

"Well, first of all, I never offered the frescoes to Dumbarton Oaks," he replied, directly contradicting the sworn testimony of Gary Vikan in Indianapolis. "I merely asked Vikan for his advice. And Dikmen's cover story about how he had discovered the frescoes in Anatolia, not Cyprus, was by no means incredible, as Vikan seemed to suggest."

And what about the most thrilling part of all *Cyprus v. Goldberg*—the part in Walter Hopps's deposition where Petsopoulos, in his anger at Dikmen's supposed lies, throws a decanter into the Turk's fireplace?

"It was a very acrimonious discussion," said Petsopoulos.

"But did you throw a decanter?" I persisted.

I heard him smother a laugh. "It was really very acrimonious. I'm sure that I threw many things."

Citing Savo's sworn statement to Peg Goldberg's lawyer, I asked him if it was true that a Montenegrin named Savo Kujundzic had retrieved from his house, in the late summer of 1989, antiquities consigned to him by Aydin Dikmen.

"I have never had anything on consignment from Mr. Dikmen," he replied. "Many years ago he sent me some photos of pieces, but they didn't interest me. And I don't know any Montenegrins at all." Petsopoulos thought for a moment or two, and then added, with emphatic gentleness, "I don't want to say that this Montenegrin was lying. Perhaps he was introduced to someone else named Petsopoulos."

The following year—that is to say, in early 1993—Petsopoulos, after a furious behind-the-scenes struggle, returned the icon of Saint John Prodrome to the Church of Cyprus, receiving in return a formal expression of the Church's gratitude. Two unconnected sources, one based on Cyprus, the other in London, informed me that he had secretly received a payment of £8,000 from the church.

In February 1992, Vassos Karageorghis also ran into heavy weather when Michael Kyprianou rose in the Greek Cypriot parliament to denounce him for allowing more than fourteen thousand artifacts to be exported during his tenure as director of the Antiquities Department. "Those who were supposed to be the guardian angels of our cultural heritage signed it away," said Kyprianou. At a hearing later that month, Kyprianou berated Karageorghis to his face for having turned a deaf ear to a formal request that he testify at the trial in Indianapolis. "We told you that your presence was necessary," Kyprianou said. "And you, sir, told me that you had to go to various universities and could not postpone these trips. Isn't it true?"

"Yes," Karageorghis replied. "I was not told that it would be the end of the world."

On reading a transcript of this remarkable exchange, I looked up the notes of my own interview with Karageorghis. He had said to me: "I informed my government that I was ready to testify on twenty-four hours' notice, but no official requested me to do so."

All during 1992 I kept in touch with Michel. He told me he had proof that Peg had known just what the mosaics were when she bought them, and that he was about to send me a crucial document; but the document never arrived. After a while I asked him about it, and he told me he'd lent all his papers to a journalist in Los Angeles, who had put them in the trunk of his car.

"He told me someone broke into his trunk," said Michel, with a snort of disbelief. "As if a car thief would be interested in my papers."

Michel also denied all Savo's allegations against him—most heatedly the claim that he had produced a pseudo-Dikmen at the Geneva airport. As for his own charges that his former bodyguards—Marko, Draža, and Hans—were involved in extortion, the Amsterdam police informed me that none of the three had ever been indicted, much less convicted, though in early 1991 a "racketeer" named Dujo had indeed been murdered in that city, by a person or persons unknown.

Often Michel could be hard to find. First he was in Holland, then in the United States. He said he was secretly collaborating with the DEA and the FBI, and, in fact, he was spotted several times in the company of a well-known and particularly inept FBI agent who'd recently been transferred from New York to Indianapolis. Then one day he called me from St. Louis. He told me he'd rented a mansion on Lindell Boulevard and bought himself a Rolls and hired some Ethiopian servants; he was about to open a wonderful new auction house that would outshine Selkirk's. He'd got his hands on a Rembrandt and an El Greco and secured major backing from some local millionaires. Yet not long afterward, he rang me from the Plaza Hotel, in New York, to report that he'd had to beat it out of St. Louis in a hurry. "The whole thing kind of blew up in my face," he said cheerfully.

"How come?"

"It was Bob—Fitzgerald. That guy is my worst enemy."

"He was in St. Louis, too?"

"Of course. He has connections there."

"And?"

"You know Bob. He can be very persuasive."

"Meaning?"

"Well, there are some things that you just don't do," he said, waiting a moment for his outrage to sink in. "I mean, really. Like warning the police—warning Interpol."

A few days later, I talked to Bob, who'd already moved from St. Louis back to Indianapolis.

"You called the police on Michel?" I asked.

"Hell no, I did not. Jesus, he said that? Let me tell you, Michel walked out of St. Louis with a million bucks. I put him in touch with big lawyers, big businessmen, but once he was all set up, he forgot who Bob Fitzgerald was. He says he admires Bob Fitzgerald so much, Bob is his big brother, and then he goes and bad-mouths me behind my back. Let me tell you, the only time he's friends with me is when he needs a grubstake."

In the meantime, I'd got an inkling of what had actually happened in St. Louis. A front-page story about Michel van Rijn appeared in the March 11 *St. Louis Post-Dispatch,* and the man who'd rented him the house on Lindell Boulevard wrote me a letter (much later, he also talked to me over the phone). Apparently Michel had moved into the house at the drop of a hat, installed a $25,000 gym on the third floor, and in the middle of the principal salon built a huge glass case in which to display his collection of toys, including his rare Ken and Barbie dolls. His way of life impressed the natives. He induced a local businessman to pay $650,000 for a "Rembrandt" and an "El Greco," both of dubious authenticity, and also showed a "Leonardo Madonna" to two well-placed museum people. (The owner of the mansion, who knew something about Italian art, saw the "Leonardo" and suspected it was actually a pastiche by Settimio Giampetri, a modern Italian painter.) Van Rijn also got a wealthy St. Louis candy and cigarette distributor (who, as it happened, had pleaded guilty about three years earlier to violating a federal money-laundering statute) to float him a big loan—according to some accounts, it exceeded $500,000. But then things began to go wrong. The manager of the sporting-goods store that had sold Michel the gym told the *Post-Dispatch,* "I was [at the mansion] one day and he was about to write me a check when he got a phone call. He said, 'I can no longer talk to you, something very bad has happened and I have to leave.'

He never wrote the check. I was there later to reclaim our equipment and there was a tailor who was owed nine thousand dollars, a picture framer owed sixteen hundred dollars, a poor painter he owed money to, the florist. A customs guy was there talking about three forgeries."

Van Rijn had both borrowed and spent huge sums of money all over town, and in the end, the businessman who bought the "Rembrandt" and the candy distributor and the United States Customs Service and a whole troop of bill collectors and repo men launched a sort of cavalry charge against him. On the night of February 29, the creditors and the agents converged on the driveway of Michel's rented mansion, where they found a van ready to roll, packed with his most valuable possessions—paintings, a slot machine, vintage toys, Mickey Mouse dolls. Van Rijn himself was nowhere to be found, but when the phone rang and a policeman picked up the receiver, his voice came on the other end of the line saying he was away on business and asking please what had happened to his van.

The strange thing was that one of the angry men standing in the driveway that night was Bob Fitzgerald. He soon phoned Peg, whom he hadn't contacted in months, to claim that van Rijn had "screwed him royally." He didn't offer any details, but Peg had heard rumors that Bob was still doing plenty of business with van Rijn on the sly, and she told me she suspected that their big blow-up was "mostly smoke and mirrors."

When I talked to Bob myself, he said, "I haven't had anything to do with Michel since St. Louis, where he screwed two guys out of a ton of money. In a way, he screwed me, too, because he told me he wasn't doing any business there."

"So you've cut no deals with him since St. Louis?"

"None. The last time he called here I hung up on him. Let me tell you something—he was out to screw somebody with those mosaics, and he decided he disliked Peg more than he disliked me. They'd developed some sort of weird animosity toward each other. If she'd listened to me, and not been so greedy, we'd have sold the mosaics for ten million. I had a few potential customers, and it was I who knew Geza von Habsburg and had put her in touch with Geza. But she wanted to give Geza a peanut, and believe me, you do not do this to Geza von Habsburg, so Geza turned around and dumped her. She should have let me handle it, but no, she wants to run to New York and play the big dealer. Hey, I don't try to play doctor, do I? Do I try to work in a hospital and give lobotomies? I don't say I wanted credit for the deal, I didn't need my name all over it. Use any name you want. Donald Duck, for Chrissake!"

I knew Bob had had a hard time selling art in Indianapolis after the publicity from the mosaics trial, and now all his frustration and disgust seemed to be rising to the surface. He sputtered furiously on, and then suddenly I realized he was telling me that Aydin Dikmen had never sold Peg a thing. It was Michel van Rijn, he was saying, who had sold the mosaics to her.

"I found this out later from a certain person in Amsterdam," he said. "Michel knew a man who owned a restaurant in Geneva and he had this man go and rent a room at the InterContinental. I believe I never met the real Dikmen, I met the phony Dikmen, and I'll bet you the phony Dikmen flipped his share of the money right back to Michel."

"You mean Dikmen never even came to Geneva?"

"Hey, who's Dikmen? I only know that a phony Dikmen took the money from me and left. I didn't ask for his ID. So I figure Michel got every last cent. And anyway, if a real Dikmen exists, which I'm not sure of, he would have gotten no more than one hundred and fifty Deutsche marks for all four pieces—Michel's a very tight buyer, you know."

Then, feeling very silly—suspecting, in fact, that Bob might be feeding me a story derived circuitously from myself—I said, "Bob, there's a Turk in Munich called Dikmen who's been saying this all along."

"Well, I believe Michel did screw Dikmen. Michel thinks kindness is weakness. I can't get along with people like that. And now because of him a lot of people around here don't want to know I exist. Bob *who*?"

"Bob, why don't you leave Indianapolis? Why don't you go someplace else?"

"I can't, I can't. I've got Evan here," he said. "I've got my little boy."

I faxed Michel, who was at a secret location, and he called me back. When I told him of my talk with Bob, he responded with cool amusement. "Bob got a huge cut out of the mosaics deal," Michel said through an audible yawn. "So what's he complaining about? Frankly, I had trouble getting *my* cut out of *him,* and it was I who masterminded the deal. The one flaw in my scheme was that I couldn't go in person to Geneva, where the money was—for that I would have needed a false passport—and when Bob came back from Geneva to the Amsterdam Marriott, where I was staying, he offered me a suitcase with only fifty thousand Swiss francs in it. Well, I tell you, I just picked up the suitcase with the money in it and threw it right out the window." There was a pause, illuminated by a vision of the banknotes fluttering down over the park in front of the Marriott, fluttering down over the tulips and the sidewalk café.

"Look, in the past I enjoyed working with Bob," Michel went on, "but now I have come to see that it was basically a business relationship. And it's over. Bob keeps you on your toes, he could stab you in the back any minute—that's the fun of working with him—but as for his tales of his life as a smuggler, well, now I am going to tell you the most heroic thing he ever did. Are you ready? Okay: it was smuggling out of South America these little green birds—"

"Parakeets?"

"Parakeets. He had a bird shop with his friend Lynn Harris in L.A., and that's all they ever smuggled; that's it. The stuff my father got from Bob out of Buenos Aires came straight through Dutch customs."

I was sure Michel's claims would infuriate Bob, but that wasn't my business anymore; I was out of it now, I was saying goodbye to them all. I had only one final question for Michel, a question that had been nagging at my mind ever since our last meeting, in The Hague.

"Michel," I said, "at that party in The Hague, when you were getting so tight, what did you mean when you said that things were 'good' between us, and that we were going to 'make a fight'?"

"Well, not a physical fight," he said, laughing, "not a fistfight or anything. I just felt that you were too serious, too uptight, and that's why I was trying to get you drunk. You were so tense, like a person in a

· 219 ·

harness, and I wanted you to appreciate the humor of it all, not to undervalue me, not to think I care only about money."

"The reason I was so tense," I said huffily, "was that I thought—"

"I know, I know, you thought I was armed, and also you were trying to get in touch with those stupid Yugoslavs behind my back. You think I didn't know that? You think I don't keep tabs on people? You were just trying to do your job, I didn't take it personally—in fact, I don't see why you didn't ask me where to find that garbage. I know all their places, I know all their clubs, I would have been happy to tell you about it. But I don't think you would have enjoyed meeting them, and frankly, they are still out hunting for me, which is why I've left Holland and moved to where I am now."

"Which is where?"

"It's a nice place, very refined, very genteel. A little provincial, maybe. But we're happy here."

And where were those missing mosaics? At times I thought I knew. Aydin had this, Marko and Draža and Hans had that, Savo and Aydin and Mehmet had an arrangement worked out, maybe Peg had bought into an apostle or two. At various times, pieces were sighted in Amsterdam, in Vienna, in a boonker in northern Cyprus; Peg told me that they had all been acquired by Savo and were "safely vaulted" in Switzerland; and then, one day, I realized that I would never find out who had them. How could I? What sort of document would prove it? What photograph? And even if someone were to take me to a bank vault and let us in with a key and stand there with his arms around those priceless treasures, how would I know they were actually his? How could I be sure that they didn't in reality belong to the man outside, the man leaning on the wall of the bank reading *Die Zeit*?

Soon after I returned home from Cyprus, in October 1991, I'd called Savo and asked how he was getting on with Aydin.

"Aydin is here in Munich, but won't help," Savo had said. "He prove that he is one wery bad little man. He call me from public telephone about the lady, what lady want. He say he is in Turkey. I say, 'I know you call from here, not Turkey.' And he answer, '*Nein*! My coins for telephone is out. Bye-bye.'"

Unlike so many other people, Savo had never seemed obsessed with the mosaics; he had never been a Kanakariá junkie. Now, on the phone, he abruptly changed the subject. He wanted to talk about the correct diet for children—no German hormones!—and the horrors of war in the former Yugoslavia. Clearly his friendship with Aydin was over.

By now Peg had become really fond of Savo—perhaps too fond, I figured, to pay much heed to Ahmet's bold claim that the Montenegrin, in the early days of his association with her, had lied to her about visiting Cyprus and had pocketed the traveling funds she'd given him. So I told Savo Ahmet's story point-blank—about the meeting being in Istanbul, not Cyprus, and about Ahmet's having to pay the bill at the Pera Palas—and as I finished I realized that Savo was moaning.

"Oh God, oh God!" he said, his voice pitched between despair and mad laughter. "Is true I go to Istanbul, yes. I remember is coming there one clochard, with not one penny, in thousand-year-old suit, seat all shiny, not one copper for food. Is coming with friend the museum director, who has no briefcase, only plastic bag from supermarket, to hold his proofs. For them I buy prepaid tickets, room in hotel, terrible Turkey food, so in restroom three days I am sitting. Oh God, oh God! Tell this clochard from Savo to shut up!"

"But, Savo," I said, "what about Ahmet's statement that you never went to Cyprus—that you pocketed Peg's money for the trip?"

"Is not true, for sure. I was in Cyprus two, three months before Ahmet is coming out from the jail. *Later,* I meet Ahmet, Mehmet, and shit-Aydin in Istanbul. I pay for everything. Aydin say, 'This is good people, I get good price for you,' but Ahmet say, 'I don't show all,' and Mehmet say, 'No proofs before money.' Mehmet visit me in Munich. He get from me twenty thousand dollars altogether."

"And these are the thousands of dollars you spent so you could legally sell the mosaics you claim to possess?"

"*Ja.* Aydin say, 'Buy nice clothes for Mehmet,' but what does Mehmet give me in exchange? Nothing. *Nothing!*"

After hearing this, I formed a plan. I figured that if Savo really did have the mosaics, he might sell them back to the Church of Cyprus at a price acceptable to both parties. I spoke to the Cypriot Minister of Communications, Demos Christou, who expressed interest in my suggestion: though the Church did not care to buy back what it regarded as its own property, Christou intimated that somehow the money might be found. My strategy was to get Peg to encourage Savo to meet with a Cypriot representative; if the deal came off, she would receive a letter from the Church thanking her for her help and absolving her of any ill will in the Kanakariá affair. She responded enthusiastically. "That letter," she said, "would make me whole again."

But what about Savo himself? He sounded guarded, sarcastic, on the phone, and responded to my queries with teasing equivocations. Then, unexpectedly, he offered to sell a single small mosaic hand back to the Cypriots as a confidence-building measure. I assumed he was referring to the Hand of Mary from the fragment with the Hand and Feet; yet reviewing photos of the Kanakariá mosaics taken in the church before the theft, I discovered, with a spine-tingling sensation, an isolated hand (probably that of an archangel) in a badly damaged section of the mosaic cycle to the right of the boy Jesus. At no time during the Indianapolis trial or in the newspaper had anybody mentioned this second hand, so Savo once again seemed privy to some very detailed information about the missing pieces; and reviewing Ronald Faulk's deposition, I found that he had seen some "little, little" mosaics on the walls of Aydin Dikmen's Munich apartment. Discreetly I began to urge Savo to make a deal with the Cypriots, and Peg told me that she, too, was "working on" him. At first we seemed to be succeeding, and then, gradually, Savo backed off. Something about my own role bothered him. Why, he wondered, did I find Michel van Rijn so perversely entertaining? Why had I never managed to contact Marko, Draža, and Hans? Whose side was I on, anyway? Savo was not the sort to bear a grudge, but he obviously couldn't rid himself of the suspicion that I was a dubious character.

By late 1992 I was tracing Savo's phone calls back to a most unlikely location—a sportswear firm in the Swiss textile-producing town of St. Gallen, near Zurich. Apparently he moved around constantly, almost as constantly as I did, yet despite various people's insinuations that he was some sort of gangster, I never came across the slightest indication that he was. Basically, his character was festive, unthreatening. Of course, I remembered his claim to have access to the Mummy of Saint Lazarus, which hadn't exactly enhanced his believability, but when I asked Peg about it she said, "He was wrong about that—he told me so himself. Those are the bones of Saint Barnabas. Savo isn't a biblical scholar, you know." Yet if I continued to put down much of Savo's quirkiness to sheer temperament, he had become unforgiving toward me, and unable, I felt, to discern what I was like. By the spring of 1993 he was refusing to speak to me, and the people at the Swiss textile firm claimed never to have heard of him. He had vanished from my life forever, and with him all hope that I would recover the missing mosaics for Cyprus or secure that healing letter for Peg.

All this while I had never stopped trying to talk to Aydin Dikmen. My desire stemmed in part from a need to reassure myself that there was such a person, and in part from my obligation to hear his views about the mosaics case in order to write about him fairly. But my contact with him was tenuous—a matter of roundabout messages, unanswered letters, and slammed-down telephone receivers.

It was a source of amusement to me that Tom Kline, Cyprus's former attorney, still argued that he didn't exist. "Look, I'm willing to believe there's someone out there with his name or alias, but that really isn't saying very much," he insisted. "Do you remember that Le Carré novel—I think it was *Tinker, Tailor, Soldier, Spy*—where one of the operatives in the field says to Control, 'Tell me what identities you have available.' Well, I think Dikmen is just such an 'identity'—a made-up character with a phony or largely phony background. And from what you tell me, there are signs that this 'identity' is now being rapidly and carefully phased out."

The thought had often struck me that certain of Dikmen's characteristics were mutually contradictory or just plain impossible. Everyone said that he was fabulously rich, yet he drove a Mitsubishi and his family lived in a small middle-class flat in an unfashionable district of Munich. Everyone said that he owned a ship-scrapping yard in Turkey—it was supposed to be in the coastal town of Aliağa, near Izmir— yet his business activities allowed him months of spare time in which to accumulate antiquities and attempt amateur restorations. He had told Savo that he adored vernacular architecture, that he had rebuilt whole sections of Istanbul, but the only person who had actually done that was a famous Turkish preservationist named Çelik Gülersoy, whom I actually knew slightly and who had nothing in common with the Dikmen identity.

Despite these contradictions, however, most of the circumstantial evidence suggested that a single person had in fact directed the looting of Byzantine Cyprus after the Turkish invasion of 1974. A man calling himself Aydin Dikmen had first attracted international notice in the late 1960s in connection with certain thefts from the great excavation of Çatal Hüyük, in Anatolia, when he had boasted to two British journalists, Kenneth Pearson and Patricia Connor, that some of the most attractive artifacts from the site had ended up in his house. He was then a young technical draftsman and part-time jazz drummer living in Konya, and he proudly invited the two writers to visit his private museum. (Already he probably knew how to draw, in the insipid art-school manner featured in his promotional material of the 1980s, and it may be that he was already writing with his trademark calligraphic hand.) In 1963 the Turkish minority in Cyprus withdrew into fortified enclaves, and exploiting the general disorder, the man called Dikmen began to develop useful contacts on the island. He met Ali Mehmet Ali, the daring smuggler and guerrilla fighter; he met the powerful antiquities merchant Yekta Remzi. After the Turkish invasion of 1974, Dikmen stepped up his buying and smuggling activities, and in 1977 a trunkload of valuable icons, discovered on its way into Yugoslavia, was traced by the Turkish police back to an associate of Dikmen's in the Grand Bazaar. The man's name was Atilla Önder, and for all I know, he still shuttles between Turkey and Cyprus on Dikmen's behalf. (I have looked for him in the bazaar, but haven't found him.) In 1977 the police also raided Dikmen's villa in Konya, but he escaped and bribed his way back into good standing. In fact, he was and remains a master at bribery: he understood that in a country like northern Cyprus the trick was to pay off petty officials, impoverished wardens, and village headmen—people who could be bought for almost nothing and couldn't effectively turn on him; it was not necessary to buy cabinet ministers, many of whom had the reputation of being upright Kemalist types. Yet when the Turkish Cypriot police finally arrested Dikmen, in 1982, and had him arraigned in the port of Kyrenia, he didn't hesitate to fly his wife in from Germany so she could deposit a tidy douceur in the judge's bank account.

I never learned when Dikmen set up shop in Munich, but I did discover how he spirited many of his stolen icons into that city; names mentioned there as belonging to persons who worked for him matched names that Turkish Cypriot policemen had seen written on the address labels of packages intercepted at the Lefkoşa airport. One of them was the German name, or alias, of the operator popularly known as the Old Man. The Old Man, who is now dead (perhaps "dead" is a better way to put it), was very helpful to Dikmen and, incredibly enough, even put some of Dikmen's people through a fresco-restoration course at the Dörner Institute; it was he, too, I believe, who abstracted Dikmen's file from the archives of the Munich Prosecutor's office. The most amazing feature of Dikmen's operation, though, was the way he availed himself of Greek Cypriot propaganda. The Greeks had convinced themselves that the looting of Cyprus was a planned government project, a deliberate chauvinist orgy, so they didn't bother looking for an ordinary non-ideological criminal ring directed from abroad. Yet actually it was almost certainly Dikmen's team that stripped many of the most important Byzantine churches in Cyprus of their paintings and mosaics: Lysi, Kanakariá, Ayios Giorgios, Ayios Varnavas, Panayia Theotokos, the Armenian Church, and the great Antiphonitis monastery. I believe that the same team, or a brother team, also ransacked Ayios Mamas, in Morphou, stealing the mortal remains of Saint Mamas, whom Savo was later to confuse with Saint Lazarus, then Barnabas. Though it is possible, even probable, that Dikmen was not physically present at most of these operations, the scent of his money seems to have triggered them. There is some evidence that the guerrilla fighter Ali Mehmet Ali put Dikmen in touch with Mehmet Rasih Savarona—the Mehmet I knew—some time before the Kyrenia Castle robbery, and whether or not Mehmet was really responsible for that crime, Dikmen walked away with quite a few prize items, some of which later found their way to Michel van Rijn and Yanni Petsopoulos and the auction block at Sotheby's. All in all, it is no exaggeration to say that Aydin Dikmen of Konya, the man who doesn't exist, is the most destructive art thief to appear in Europe since the end of World War II.

There are some fictive events, conversations or meetings, that replay so often in our minds that they slip in unnoticed among the crowd of our memories, assume the guise of reality, take on a life of their own. They are dreams, mere wisps of smoke, but they have beautiful, compelling shapes, and in the end seem more substantial than anything else, rising higher than ourselves, until in the end they look down on us—which is why we call them tall tales.

For months I have been haunted by such a tall tale

or dream, a dream in which at last I have no need to pretend to believe the person who is talking to me, no need to detect what secret benefit my bandied words will bring him, no need to wonder what emotions are masked by his unfading smile. In my tall tale none of these traps can possibly be set, because this time I myself am the teller, I am the conjuror, and I waft up smoke in great clouds. In my dream or tall tale I am in Munich once again, only this time it is autumn, the streets are awash in rain, and reflections of buildings and headlights and the twilight sky swirl along together in the gutters. I have boarded a tram, a dream tram that winds concertina-like toward the center of the city, its few passengers silent, unsmiling, heedless of the disembodied voice that announces the successive stops, blind to the forgotten black umbrella hooked over the handrail, its way of sliding this way and that like some frightened creature, a sprite in widow's weeds.

In my tall tale I get off at the Hauptbahnhof and pick my way through the puddles toward a pedestrian street lined by long, nondescript buildings, one of which I enter—a hotel—and seat myself at the bar in the pink-and-cream lounge, under the coved, softly lighted ceiling, where I await the arrival of my informant. It is only after several minutes, after several troubled glances at my watch, that I become aware that a grizzled, bespectacled gentleman, well dressed and well shod, has been observing me from the depths of an alcove, studying my appearance with a look that is really a question. In my tall tale that look, when seen from close up—from the other side of the table at which I now seat myself—is unusually intelligent and filled with a palpable anguish, so that even to glance at the aging sufferer seems a pitiless exacerbation of his pain. His skin is at once murky and colorless, an unfired-pottery hue, and I notice his black briefcase with its embossed gold initials and almost microscopic stitching, and beside it his folded copy of the financial section of *Süddeutsche Zeitung*. In my tall tale he makes the offer of a cigarette, which I decline, and then signals the barman to bring us a pair of cognacs. With profuse apologies, he accords me half an hour of his time, and we settle upon French as the vehicle of the interview, for he has the greatest admiration for the French language, the "most melodious and expressive" in Europe.

"So what is it," he asks me, "doctor or mister—I'm sorry—that you wish to know?"

"You needn't call me doctor, just Dan will do."

"As you wish. And how may I be of service?"

"It has to do with the lady."

A secretive look comes into his eyes; he says nothing, so I begin my indictment.

"Your name was divulged to the press in May 1989, about the time of the trial in Indianapolis. Is that correct?"

"I suppose so." He is uncomfortable; his fingertips drum on the table.

"Well, ever since then, either in person or through various intermediaries, you have been telling the lady that the former Cypriot antiquities minister, Dr. Vassos Karageorghis, was acting in collusion with you. Correct?"

"Please continue."

"You are known to be a man in touch with his instincts. Well, I believe those instincts told you, as soon as you met the lady, that she was inordinately proud of her intelligence, that she would never admit to herself that she had made a ghastly mistake in buying four of the Kanakariá mosaics. So you encouraged her to believe she could win her case against the Cypriots. You encouraged her to believe that Ahmet or Mehmet was in possession of documents proving her case. Of course, this was an illusion, a mirage that had to be kept aloft as long as she had an appeal pending, as long as there was a chance she might settle out of court with the Cypriots and turn against you, possibly with the aid—and this was a thought that you could not have relished—of Interpol or the Munich police. So, like any shrewd swindler, you had her coming back for more, you had her eagerly awaiting her redemption. It was brilliant—a master stroke."

In my tall tale the Turkish gentleman tosses his head back during this recital and gazes upward, like a small child refusing food, then trains his tormented eyes upon me.

"Your rambles about Europe, Mr. Dan, have afforded me much amusement," he says, in his B-movie lingo. "You have gone here and there, a little everywhere, and you have gathered many facts—many facts, sir, but no real information. You have never considered the sort of people with whom you were talking, you have never considered the quality of your sources. And for a person like yourself, well, quality should be everything. This Michel van Rijn! Really! And the lady, too—no, permit me to continue—the lady behaved very badly. In the end, you go to Cyprus, you talk to Turkish people, but what class of people you seem not to understand. I cannot tell you your business, sir, but I sense that you fail to discriminate. We Turkish people are not all alike, and many of us are very artistic."

"That I would be the last to deny, Aydin Bey. But your own artistry, if one must call it that, is of a very different nature. And the peculiar form of redemption you were offering the lady—you put quite a price tag on it, didn't you? You also decided, apparently rather early, that the proceeds from the sale of the evidence ought to go to Ahmet or Mehmet. Exactly why I'm not sure. Maybe you owed them money, maybe they knew too much about you—in a way, it doesn't really matter. What does matter is that you convinced them they could make a killing in a deal with a woman they believed to be fantastically rich. You played both ends against the middle. But what papers did they have that would hold up in court? In my opinion, none whatsoever. Now, I don't say that Karageorghis never met you, Aydin Bey, and I don't say that he never bought anything from you—I'm not in a position to know. What I do say is that even if these things happened, which is far from certain, the chances are infinitesimally small that either you or anyone else ever possessed invoices or receipts bearing both your name and his. Certainly Peg never *saw* them. And such receipts are the only thing, aside from a photo of the two of you playing tennis together or sharing a kebab, that would have interested an American judge. So your strategy has paid off, Aydin Bey. Nobody ever goes after you. You are immune!"

All along he has been drumming the table, but now he ceases, and his gaze calmly engages my own. "I don't think I quite understand you, Mr. Dan. You have lost me somewhere along the way with your *mirages* and *redemptions*. Let me reply with an anecdote from the story of my people. When the Fatih conquered Constantinople—you know who I mean by the Fatih?"

"Of course."

"So charming of you to know a little of our history! Well, when he conquered Constantinople, he went into the Cathedral of Hagia Sophia, where the Patriarch and the bishops and the nobility had sought refuge, and he tried to quiet their fears. He told them that he would honor them and respect their religion, and that they would not come to any harm. Then he saw one of his own soldiers, off to the side in the shadows, prying a gold tile off a wall, and he grew very angry. He had the man brought before him. 'Are you a man?' he said to the thief. 'A man does not destroy! A man builds.' Now, I ask you—you are a writer—is this not the most wonderful definition of a man? *A man builds!*"

"And that is what you were doing in the Church of Kanakariá?" I exclaim, enraged by his venomous fawning. "You have a very odd notion of what it is to build, Aydin Bey."

"A realistic notion, I believe." He fixes me with a stare, then plucks down one of his lower eyelids with a finger, as though to say: Open your eyes. "I can see that you do not appreciate me, and I regret that I have not made my point. I am not skilled in the techniques of communication. But when I hear you talking I say to myself, 'There is an American speaking.' You have a great country, sir. I myself was in the American Hospital in Istanbul for my kidney stones—what wonderful care, and what doctors! But in other matters you are very naïve, one of our young girls would laugh at you. Oh, please do not glare at me like that! Your little joke about my making off with the Kanakariá mosaics betrays your innocence about conditions on the island of Cyprus. Even if by and large the Turkish Army behaved correctly, it is still true that every regiment in the world has its ruffians, every village has its rowdies, and those mosaics would not have survived without my intervention. Have you ever seen a great church converted into a shelter for sheep, sir? Have you ever seen mildew and rising damp inching their way toward a thousand-year-old fresco? Believe me, for people like ourselves this is a very sad sight. So please understand: I am not the destroyer of those mosaics, sir—I am their savior! I am the savior of the image of God."

"And probably the destroyer of two Kanakariá roundels," I say, trying to contain my fury, "because there are at least two in the old photos that have never resurfaced anywhere. And I know about your so-called restoration activities, Aydin Bey. They are virtually confined to the concoction of a pair of ridiculous fakes."

"Concoction? That is a painful word. Who has told you this—was it Benjamin?"

"Yes, it was Benjamin. Your dear old friend."

He shrugs. "You seem to think that Benjamin knows where the so-called missing pieces are—Saint Andrew, Saint Thomas, and the Feet. Do you think he is a credible person?"

"It's not my job to determine who is a credible person," I say, "but to determine whether certain statements are credible."

"And you believe what Benjamin says merely because he has also asserted that Mehmet and Ahmet and I swindled him out of some money—out of twenty thousand dollars, to be exact? His confession or pseudo-confession of this loss makes the rest of his claims believable—that is the extent of your psychology? You do not answer. Well then, tell me, has Benjamin shown you the missing pieces or told you his asking price?"

"No, he hasn't."

"I see. So he has stated that he has the pieces, or has access to the pieces, but at the same time he is not interested in selling them to you—"

"To the Cypriots."

"Of course, to the Cypriots. Excuse me! You never buy anything for yourself. So he advertises pieces that he refuses to sell. A most original marketing strategy! Do you know what I make of it, or what I would make of it if I were you? I would conclude that either he is an outrageous impostor or that he does not find you, or your statements—for me they are one and the same—sufficiently credible. He does not trust you to be a disinterested broker."

In my tall tale he falls silent here, swirls his brandy contemplatively, takes a long sip. He looks down for a moment, then says, "Excuse me, but all this while I have been wishing to ask you something. Your name, Mr. Dan—what does it mean?"

"Aydin, that's a rug seller's line, and I haven't a clue what it means."

"No? A pity. Because all names do mean something, you know. My name, in Turkish, means moonlight. Turkish children sing a lovely song to Ay Dede—Granddaddy Moon. And I have tried to live up to my name and be a little like the moon. Sometimes nobody can find me—that has been your own experience, which I regret—and sometimes I am there for all to see: curators, collectors, prime ministers. You understand, I have no wish to make a mystery of my doings, but sometimes it simply happens that way. The side of me in the light is at peace with the side in the shadow. I know how the world sees me, and the question that I would ask of you is: Do you? I would tend to suspect, if what you are telling me about Benjamin is true, that perhaps he sees something about you that you have not seen. And this is bad for you. Like this you cannot deal, you cannot buy, you cannot sell, you cannot even approach somebody on behalf of somebody else—you are *hors de combat*."

"I have never wanted to deal."

"Yes, but we are all dealers, Mr. Dan! You, as a writer, deal in questions and answers, yet I have noticed that you never ask the questions you intended to ask—you seem to mislay or forget them. Your great burning question, for example—why have you not asked it?"

"All right, then, I will." I have never been particularly receptive to criticism, and by now I am trembling with rage. "Tell me, Aydin Bey, do you have the missing pieces?"

"I prefer," he says, in a sort of stage whisper that ends in a guffaw, "not to answer that question."

"Of course you prefer! None of you people ever prefers to answer any question."

He shrugs again. "May I offer you some advice, Mr. Dan? Never be tempted to appropriate another man's identity for your own allegorical purposes, as you have done with me. You will corrupt your imagination if you do so. And stop struggling to conclude your little story, to pass through the last door and stand in the last chamber that is hidden amid all the other chambers. You have chased through the Grand Bazaar and found nothing and no one; why do you suppose that your tale has an end? We who love beautiful things wish to repair everything, all vessels, all lamps, and all carpets, but some damaged carpets can never be repaired, because we cannot rediscover their pattern. Is that so terrible a thing?"

He mops his brow with his handkerchief and glances furtively around the empty lounge. "I'm afraid that a pressing matter now calls me away," he says, downing what remains of his cognac and reaching for his briefcase. "It has been a pleasure for me to meet you, and I hope I have been of some help. It remains only for me to make you a small present so that you may remember me warmly, for I do not think we shall meet again."

Then he rises and takes out of his briefcase a small bag made of coarse jute, fastened at the top by a drawstring and weighed down by an irregular lump, and in my tall tale my heart jumps. As he places the bag on the table I hear a rattling sound as of many small stones jumbled together.

I undo the string and peer into the bag, but in my tall tale there is too little light for me to make out what is there. So I empty the contents onto the table: a pile of tiny square tiles, ocher, rose madder, dull blue, tarnished gold. They glitter dimly before my eyes.

"Tesserae," he says. "That is all I have left. Perhaps you can do something with them."

"Where did you get these?" I ask bitterly. "From your 'building' activities?"

"From a shop in Nicosia," he says in my tall tale.

"They were sold to the shop by thieving old priests who had picked sacred mosaics to pieces. It was the gold they were keen on—from the halos. These Greeks!"

By now, Peg and I have gone our separate ways. She is irked, I feel, by my role as professional onlooker. She is disappointed that I was unable to discover more information that would have supported her account of the mosaics story. And she is saddened by my lingering doubts over the wisdom of her great purchase. Yet who would not be troubled by the degree to which she unwittingly collaborated with her deceivers? Even if one can charitably dismiss from one's mind the thought that she may have knowingly bought stolen goods, isn't it also true that she must somehow have sensed that she was being primed for an illicit deal? After all, in her testimony she remembered that Michel van Rijn had been convicted of forgery; that Bob Fitzgerald had mentioned the mosaics to her a few years before their trip to Holland; that he said he had talked to Michel about her before that trip; and that Ronald Faulk had gone to see Aydin Dikmen shortly before her arrival in Holland. She had participated with them in a meaningless general bill of sale with a bogus purchase price. Much suggests that in some perilously passive way she played along with them, unable to divine their stratagem but convinced that there was some reward in it for her. It seemed that the compartments in her mind had stopped communicating with one another, like those of a damaged submarine.

Peg tried many times to convince me that she had

no feeling of having been manipulated. *Of course* Bob had mentioned her to Michel, just as he had mentioned Michel to her—what of it? Weren't they all in the same business and thus potential partners? Bob had sold many distinguished pieces to Indianapolis museums, and Michel was a folk hero in Holland. As for Faulk's initial trip to see Dikmen, what she had been given to understand at the time was that he'd made it in a last-ditch effort to secure the mosaics for *Michel*; the Dutchman had wanted the pieces for himself, and he had brokered them to Peg only in order to gain a percentage of their resale price. As for Michel's forgery conviction, it might indeed have bothered her if she hadn't been "so careful," as she put it, in her own inquiries. And the false bill of sale for $1,200,000? It had been drawn up not by her but by Faulk; it had quite surprised her at the time, but he had prevailed upon her to sign it.

However all this may be, Peg lost a big lawsuit and a lot of money: she acquired a huge debt service; she was obliged by law to pay some of Cyprus's court costs; her gallery house was long in danger of repossession; and her good name was hurt. She felt ill done by. But most of all, perhaps, she never stopped pining for her archangel.

"I still look at his photo every day," she told me a while back. "It wrenched my heart out to say goodbye to him. I must have known him before, in some other world—we were friends, I know we were. Those haunting, magical eyes! I'll never forget the moment I found out who he was—I was screaming almost hysterically to a friend, 'He's an angel! An angel!' "

Nevertheless, I detected, toward the end of my involvement in the mosaics affair, a great change in

Peg's disposition. Gone were the sighs, gone the laments, gone the scattershot attacks on almost everyone involved in the catastrophe. Her constant perception of the phoniness of others, which had at times made her seem mired in too-innocent outrage, had yielded to a new briskness, a new engagement in unfolding projects. Often she was terribly busy now, too busy to talk on the phone, or else away on business. Soon I began to hear amazing rumors about her. I heard that she had been offered part of the Sevso Treasure, an enormously valuable hoard of ancient silver whose ownership was angrily disputed, and that her aid in the dispute had been enlisted by Scotland Yard; I heard that she'd been sighted in Tadzhikistan, in the company of officials whose job it was to sell that country's rare minerals to the West. Her own business changed its name; her house remained in her possession; her credit, as far as I knew, was good. During one of our brief chats she described herself to me as a "precious-metals trader," and though I had no idea whether she was making money or merely borrowing it, I knew that like most of us she had to borrow it in order to make it, and that therefore she must possess the rarest gift a trader can have—the ability to persuade people to lend you large amounts of cash.

One day when I called her up she told me she'd just bought a car.

"What kind of car?" I asked.

"A Maserati," she answered proudly. "Used—a Biturbo. It's always been one of my heart's desires. Zero to ninety in about two-and-a-half seconds and a sharp inhale. Corners like a dream. Come out and drive it yourself sometime."

Peg was "whole again"—indeed, she was having her revenge.

I'm sure that at Peg's place the cats still scamper about. There's a new dog. There are Mendelssohn and Chopin scores on her piano. She is up to her ears in letters and faxes, in bills and invoices and contracts, and I suppose that every now and then, as she's shuffling through her files or hunting through her shelves, her eye falls upon Michel's book about icons, the one with the melancholy saint on the cover. Inside (does she bother to reread it?), there is his inscription, penned in a very swash hand: "To Peg Goldberg. Everywhere in the world, God and the Devil are at war, and their battlefield is the heart of man. Yours, Michel." And scrawled underneath is a smiling sun that sends its rays across the white page.